Herschel "Bones" Pedersen

Stories from My Life

HERSCHEL "BONES" PEDERSEN

STORIES FROM MY LIFE

HERSCHEL PEDERSEN

EDITED BY
DON NORTON AND JOANNE B. FILLMORE

New York

For additional copies visit: www.latterdaylegends.com

Send inquiries to:
Digital Legend Press and Publishing
1994 Forest Bend Dr.
Salt Lake City, UT 84121
U.S.A.

To see all of Digital Legend's titles visit
www.digitalegend.com/catalog

For info write to: info@digitalegend.com
or call toll free: 877-222-1960

Printed in the United States of America
First Printing: November 2009 (v1)

ISBN: 978-1-934537-84-8

Table of Contents

Foreword

BY GEORGE DURRANT

As I was living away from American Fork during Herschel's time there, I did not know him personally. However, I heard many stories about him which were so astounding that I wondered if anyone could really be as good as the reports that I heard of Brother Pedersen. I was told of his effectiveness in bringing a multitude of his fellow workers to the gospel light at the blast furnace of Geneva Steel plant. And his work was legendary in leading back to the fold a legion of fallen young adults.

Then, nine years ago, Herschel and I became fellow sealers in the Mt. Timpanogos Temple. Through the next few years, I observed firsthand the depth of this man's soul.

I wanted to know what was in the heart of this man that made him such a remarkable husband, father, teacher, leader and priesthood man. Selfishly, I asked him if I could come to his home, interview him, and record on tape his life's feelings and faith. Each Monday for the next several weeks I asked him questions about why he was the way he was.

We started our interview reminiscing about his boyhood on a farm where he was taught by his faithful father and loving mother. During his young years he sang in a children's choir in the Salt Lake Tabernacle. There he had a vivid impression of the truthfulness of the gospel, and that nurtured testimony has continued to be his guiding light.

Then we moved into his youth. I was spellbound as he told me story after story of his adventures. I was amused as he related to me his going into the fields in search of rooster pheasants. He carried no shotgun. Instead, with the stealth of an Indian brave, he crept up on these wily birds and caught them with his bare hands. Soon the chickens in his father's coop had been displaced by a flock of these beautiful birds. He told me of going to the canyons to catch fish. Not with a fishing pole and worms. Instead, he waded up stream in the mountain creeks, and with his big hands under the water he would slowly move against the current until he could feel the underbelly of a trout. He would move his hand forward and scoop the fish up.

Herschel and I talked of his remarkable high school and college basketball career. In high school he didn't make the team until his senior year. Even then the coach told him that his job was to play defense and to get rebounds, but he was told never to shoot or he would be taken out of the game. In the finals of the state championship the game was close. Herschel could tell that the team's only chance to win the tight game was for him to disregard the coach and take the ball and score. He did that three times and led his team to the crown. He was rewarded by being named all-state.

We discussed his romance with and marriage to Shirley. On their first date they parked. He told her to lead the two of them in prayer. He wanted a wife who knew how to pray. She passed the test. She was the perfect one for Herschel and he was the same for her.

He had a remarkable basketball career at BYU. Having just returned from his mission to Denmark and his two years in the army, he had to work his way into the starting lineup. He was sent into one game and was reporting at the scorer's table. While he waited for a time-out, the scorekeepers asked him to get down so they could see the game. Unable to get low enough, he laid his six-foot, seven-inch frame down on the floor. As he did so a large smile crossed his face. To the massive crowd he looked like he was a mile long. The fans, when they saw him lying there smiling, were greatly amused. From then on Herschel, "Bones" Pedersen was the most popular player BYU had ever had.

As we talked, I was enthralled with his insights, his love and his power as a teacher and a counselor. His humble account of his service as a missionary, bishop, mission representative of the Twelve, and mission president made me wish all Church leaders could be as he was.

His remarkable memory allowed him to learn thousands of scriptures. He can recite content, chapter and verse for every gospel principle. He can enlighten a discussion on doctrines or principle by quoting what the Church leaders from Joseph Smith to Thomas Monson have said about these truths. Herschel has the perfect blend of humility and boldness which endears him to all—even those he has reproved.

Many, desiring further light and truth, go to Brother Pedersen. He gives soul-satisfying answers. In his bounteous garden, where he, when not in the temple each morning, spends most of his spring and summer hours and entertains visitors with ideas on gardening and the gospel. He always has time for a gospel conversation or to give counsel and love to a struggling friend. Herschel has never met a person who was not his friend.

After these interviews, and in knowing Herschel, I know that his greatest quality is his willingness to serve. When the phone rings, as it does so often, and a request comes to him to speak, his reply is, "You betcha I'll come. Just tell me where and when." Once people have heard his testimony and knowledge they plead with him to come back and teach them again. Thus he is often on the road for a few blocks, or for hundreds of miles, to be with those who need a boost in their commitment to follow the Savior.

His wife understands what her husband has to give, so she willingly and lovingly either goes with him or waits at home for his return.

He often has people come to his home to be taught. Some come for an hour, some for a day and some for months. They are welcome to stay as long as they need to or desire to. Herschel and Shirley always have their door and hearts open to the needy.

As I interviewed Brother Pedersen I would go home after each session and tell my family about what he had told me that day. I longed for them and everyone else to know what an ordinary man could do who was willing to put his hand into the hand of God and give his life to strengthening others. I dreamed of a book that all could have so that they could know Herschel as I do and thus love him as I do.

I could go on for hours telling you Herschel Pedersen stories. But that is what this book is for. As you turn the pages that follow, get ready to be taught and inspired by a true servant of the Lord. Once you have come to know this man you will never again be the same.

—George Durrant

Acknowledgments

I didn't understand why George Durrant wanted to make tapes of my stories several years ago, but I agreed to do it. We spent several nights together and came up with over twenty hour-long tapes. About six months later, an old friend, Wade Fillmore, called me to say he felt impressed to urge me to make a book out of the stories I had shared with him some twenty years earlier. "Funny you should say that," I replied. "George Durrant just taped me telling stories for several hours."

Wade and his wife, Joanne, came to my house and borrowed the tapes. They made copies of the tapes and arranged for their transcription. Joanne carried the load for this project, which ended with 540 double-spaced pages, a treasure to my family. The Fillmores tried, without success, to get an editor and publisher for the book. Then they went away on two missions. Returning, they contacted me again. They asked Don Norton to assist to distill and edit the manuscript. We submitted an edited sampling of the work, but were turned down by the publisher we had chosen. Then Wade found Boyd Tuttle, a friend of one of my daughters and president of his own publishing company in New York. He agreed to publish the book using a technique he calls "real-time" publishing.

I am deeply grateful to George, who also wrote the Foreword, to Wade and Joanne for their persistence and dedicated work, to Don and Joanne for their editing work, to Boyd, who was willing to take a chance with me by publishing these stories, to Jennifer Orten who so skillfully designed and typeset the book, and to all others who have assisted in this project.

I am also deeply grateful for my beloved wife, Shirley, for her patience and encouragement, which have sustained me from the beginning of our relationship. Without her faith in me, very little of what is reported in these stories would have happened.

INTRODU

I would like first to express a few thoughts about myself—what made me what I have become and why I have done what I have done. A few experiences in my life may say best what and how I believe.

Before this world began, in what we believe to be the premortal life, our lives were planned. That is, we became acquainted with many others, and somehow we would meet these people in this mortal life in circumstances much different from those we knew before we were born. As we renew those friendships in this life, we have the agency to renew those premortal associations or to pass them by, depending on the paths we choose in mortality. Many of the little things that happen to us in life may seem neither coincidental nor miraculous, even though they may be turn out to be extraordinary.

Readers will find in my life story example after example of such seeming coincidences and miracles. Such happenings come to people who expect them and who try to live worthy to experience them. Here is one such example.

…been in New Zealand as mission president for …ays when the telephone rang at 1:30 in the morning. …ecting news of some missionary emergency we didn't even know about, I anxiously wondered to myself, "What can it possibly be at this time in the morning?"

The voice answered, "Are you President Pedersen?"

"Yes."

"How long have you been in New Zealand?"

"Three days."

The voice continued: "I am not a member of your church, but I pray and I read the Bible much. I have many questions, and no one seems to be able to answer them.

"One particular question from the Bible has troubled me for years. Three weeks ago, as I was praying, I received an answer to my prayer. I was told that if I would call this telephone number, on this day, a man named President Pedersen would answer the phone. I would be able to meet with him, and he would answer my questions."

And so it happened.

After being in New Zealand for a little over a month, I was sitting in my office one afternoon reading the many letters that came weekly from the missionaries. The phone rang, and Sister Olson, the mission secretary, answered it. "Would you speak to a nonmember on the line?" she asked me.

It so happened that the day I arrived in the mission, the former mission president had agreed that I would speak at a fireside the very first Sunday evening after my arrival. The person on the phone said he had attended the fireside and now he needed to talk to me. He didn't want to talk to the missionaries. And he wanted to come over immediately. I agreed. I could read the missionary letters later.

Dressed in a fine suit and tie, the man appeared to be a professional businessman. As we spoke, it became very apparent that he knew much more about the Church than any nonmember I had ever spoken to. He had read the Book of Mormon a number of times, and the Doctrine and Covenants as well. He had listened to many general conferences of the Church. In fact, as I listened to him, I began to suspect he might be an excommunicated member—but that proved not to be the case.

As he left, he asked for another appointment, and over the next few months, I met with him and others of his friends half a dozen times. But we never came to any conclusions.

The following visit was very different. He showed me a photograph of me. Where he had got it, I didn't ask. He proceeded to tell me that he and his friends had known for six months before I arrived that I would be the mission president (that was three months before *I* knew I would be the mission president). They also knew that I would be speaking at the fireside which they had all attended.

I then learned that they belonged to an organization they called "The Craft." Their desire was that their children join the Church, because one of the prophecies was that their children would join the Church in the third and fourth generations.

Inspirations in this life such as this one, evidence of a premortal life, come from two different sources—one from God, the other from the evil spirits we knew in those years long gone by. I believe many of the good spirits knew us and are aware of the things we were foreordained to do in this life. Thus they have knowledge of our life's plan from its beginning. When we consider something miraculous, maybe even too sacred to talk about, it may well be the result of promptings or interventions in our appointed missions or the spiritual needs of people we encounter.

Many of my experiences in working with inactive fellows at Geneva Steel certainly were the workings of the Spirit. My involvement in the sport of basketball opened many doors to bless the lives of others. My callings as elders quorum president and mission representative for the Church presented many challenges. Our mission to New Zealand was marked by an abundance of interventions such as I have just recounted.

We all read such stories and hope someday to have similar experiences, all the while wondering why we have had not had the abundance that others report. The answer is simple: Such experiences happen on the road we are all traveling. When we reach a critical junction, they simply occur—*if* we do not turn out of the way. Also, such stories may be but the final chapter in an episode we have not thought about seriously, or we may have lost sight of their real purpose or meaning, grand and miraculous though they may have been.

This is what I mean by "traveling the road" and witnessing spiritual experiences. They are not like seeing the deer in the field or the coyote trotting across the desert. These are things of great spiritual value that may go unnoticed, or even wasted, because we have not bothered to expect or recognize them.

We all enjoy the same freedom in this life and experience the same desires. Many times we'll have the opportunity to serve someone, or otherwise touch someone's life, when it may not be convenient to act. But let us remember that there is no inconvenience when we serve the Lord.

Opportunities to experience the unexplained and miraculous are many, and these are the kinds of experiences each of us hopes for. My hope is that my experiences, as I relate them in this book, will persuade Church members to listen to the promptings of the Spirit and experience the truly miraculous in their own lives.

Chapter One

Birth and Early Years

My family were "superstitious" people, if you call believing in inspiration and revelation being superstitious. The night I was born (and I've been told this story dozens of times), there was a blizzard. The doctor who was coming to the house to deliver me was late, and my mother was in distress. There was little heat in the house—we only had a little coal stove in those days—so the water had frozen in the sink, and buckets of water in the house were frozen. The only warm place was around the stove, so my mother had been brought to that room.

All the people there—including my father and grandfather—thought that Satan was trying to kill me the night I was born, trying to keep me from getting here. So they raised their arms to the square, had a prayer, and rebuked the power of the destroyer on my behalf so that I'd live and amount to something—be a good person who would represent the Church and otherwise do something worthwhile in the world. My mother almost died when I was born. The doctor told my parents, "You've got a choice: I can either save

Two sisters were yet to be born when this picture of Herschel's parents and siblings was taken in about 1939. Herschel is back row, second from left.

the baby or the mother. I can't save them both." My father said, "Do what you can. They'll both be all right."

The doctor put forceps around my head and helped me be born, though I think that process elongated my head. The doctor announced, "Well, this child's definitely got brain damage." He put his hands under my jaw and on top of my head and proceeded to crush my head back down to a somewhat normal-size skull. The family all witnessed this.

I was administered to and blessed.

Still, I wonder if I did turn out normal—and so do a lot of other people. But I did survive, and I think I turned out normal enough. Because I did live, the family always thought I would be someone special.

One day the school principal took me to his office: I was going to be made a crossing guard. You know, you wore a little bandoleer across your chest that said, "Crossing Guard." At noon, I would stand on the corner across the street from a little store and walk out with a little sign so the cars would stop and let kids cross the street.

I thought that a big honor, so I went home and told my parents how proud I was to be chosen for that responsibility. I was to start the following week.

But when I went to the principal's office the next week, instead of my being given a bandoleer, I was told that I wasn't qualified for the job. I don't remember exactly what was said, only that I now felt inferior, like I'd been rejected.

I was also self-consciously tall—taller than the other kids. When I entered first grade, I was so much taller than the rest of the kids that I was put in the sixth grade, even though I couldn't read, write, or nothing. It took the teachers half an hour to find out that compared to the other sixth graders, I was an idiot. I swear that my first day of school was four days long. Every time we went out for recess, I thought it was time to go home. It was the longest day of my life.

In elementary school I was shy and backward. I *was* a pretty good marble player. I'd go to school with three or four marbles and come home with pockets full of a hundred (I had gallon cans full of marbles).

When I was about twelve years old, something happened which my mother and father thought was significant in my life. First of all, they'd had me get my patriarchal blessing. Harold B. Lee was the president of the stake which the Poplar Grove Ward was part of, and we were in the same ward as Thomas S. Monson. Marion G. Romney and Glen Rudd—a lot of great people came from that little ward in Salt Lake City. Of course the city wasn't very big back in those days.

We were bussed the seven miles to school (my uncle was the bus driver), but the only kids I knew at school were three or four neighbors who lived up in the farming area. I didn't know any of the other thirty or so kids in my class, and that bothered me. That's when I became something of a recluse—and I stayed that way all through school. I didn't go to dances, I didn't talk to girls, I never read much. I just worked on the farm, hunted, fished and played basketball. That's all I cared about. I did always go the church.

When World War II began, only about seven families lived out where we lived on the thousands of acres of nothing but sagebrush. It was like playing Old West because we could hunt pheasants and rabbits near the house, and we could run and run for miles in the open spaces. Some readers may remember the tall and thin marshelder weeds. When they dried in the fall, they were just like spears, and that's how we used them as we explored the area.

One morning in the spring of the year, I told my mother and father (Dad was in the bishopric of the ward), "Look, if you don't mind, I'm going to start going to the other ward, and I'll go all the time. I'll never miss." The other ward heated the chapel with an old pot-bellied stove.

I'd gone there for a year and a half when President Lee announced the creation of a new ward, and my father was made the bishop. Because I'd determined to attend church so faithfully on my own, my parents thought I had a special character or some special courage. (I might go hunting rabbits early in the morning, but I was always home in time for Sunday School at 10:30 in the morning.)

As a kid, I once had to give one of those two and a half minute talks in Sunday School, and I was terrified. When I was a teacher in the priesthood, fifteen or so years old, the stake president called my parents and told them he wanted me to give a three-minute talk in stake conference. I had never been so terrified in my life! I didn't sleep for three days.

My parents helped me with my talk. I memorized every word of it, but still, when I got to the pulpit, I trembled and shook. And when I sat down, I prayed that I could get out of the building as soon as possible.

Chapter Two

Early Interest in Athletics and High School Basketball

My family lived in a rural area known as Chesterfield—it's now part of West Valley City. We went to church at the Poplar Grove Ward in Salt Lake City. When the Remington Arms plant was built on Redwood Road, houses suddenly started springing up—a lot of them shacks and such. The good pay at the plant brought people from all over, and they weren't all the "best" of people.

A new Church unit was organized, first called the Cannon Branch, off the Cannon Ward. (The branch later became a ward.) Army barracks were brought in, and during meetings we sat on chairs. Classrooms were made by dividing people up in this corner and that corner. We could no longer play with the kids in the Poplar Grove Ward because we were in a new ward. The new kids were the kids I was now going to school with.

I first became interested in athletics when I was just a young boy. The neighbor south of us had been an All-State halfback in football for Granite High School, had run the 100- and 200-yard dashes, and was the starting guard on the basketball team. Though he was a few years older than I, once when we had a spring break, he dug a high jump pit, using the soft dirt for landing. He got us running and jumping, and also playing basketball. He helped us learn to play ball before he went into the navy, and that's how we started to learn the game.

Every Sunday afternoon after morning church meetings, we boys would eat, and then from about 1:30 till five o'clock we'd go out and play some kind of sport. In the wintertime, that sport was basketball. The coach had joined the navy, but he had got us all interested in playing basketball.

Our coach was my uncle, and he didn't know any more about basketball than did the bull out in the barn, but he'd still haul us to and from games. We always lost. I played on the junior high school football, basketball, and softball teams in the ninth grade, and we had some inter-school games. In junior high school, our coach, the math teacher, had never played a game of anything in his life, yet he coached football and basketball. There were only about thirty kids in the ninth grade, so nearly every boy in the class was on the basketball team. Fortunately, we boys were pretty tall.

By my sophomore year at Granite High School, I was pretty tall—and also pretty skinny. I went out for the team but was soon cut. I could play just as well in the backyard as guys on the sophomore team, but when it came to playing under a coach, I just didn't seem to have it, even though I was one of the tallest kids in high school at six feet, seven inches. My junior year, I went out for the team, but again I had the privilege of being cut on the first round of cuts. I ended up playing for the ward basketball team.

By then, World War II had ended, our old coach again started playing ball with us a little, and he was called to be our M-Men basketball coach, even though we were sixteen- and seventeen-year-old Varsity Scouts. But after two practices, we were good enough to go undefeated the rest of the year—this because we had a coach who knew something about basketball. We kids in the ward practiced all the time.

Five of my friends did make the varsity basketball team as juniors, though I could still play as well as any of them in the backyard. Tryouts at Granite High School were not like tryouts at any other school I've ever heard of. You played in kind of an intramural league, while the coach sat and watched you. Then he'd post a list of the guys who could try out for the team. I always got to try out, but I just never got to stay on the team.

Our senior year, those of us who were always cut formed a team we called the Rinky Dinks. Reed Smith, who was on our team, had made the high school varsity team the year before.

So here we were again, now all seniors, the same ones who had tried out for the team all three years. Coach Baker saw us come in for tryouts. I said to him, "Coach, I think I can still play ball, and I love the game. I'm just here to have some fun."

He kind of smiled—we were the same five guys who had tried out every year.

Well, the five of us played that whole first week, and we went undefeated. I was averaging about eighteen to twenty points a game, even though we didn't get any coaching. Sure enough, when the coach posted his list of players to try out for the varsity team, not only was my name on the list, but the names of all five of us were on it. That was something that had never happened before, so all five of us friends got to try out for the team.

After the first week, cuts brought the team down to fifteen, and I thought for sure I'd be cut. The coach could only carry twelve players. Still I was excited, even though in practices I hadn't even been assigned a position to play, though mostly it was center or forward. I didn't know any of the coach's plays, or what had been done in high school.

One of the kids on the team, Phil Pher, who was a little smaller than I was, had been my friend all the way through high school. Then the coach announced that he was going to have to cut two more people, and then after the Friday game with Cyprus High School, he'd have to cut two more. Thursday night at practice, my friend Phil was sitting on the bench, like many of us always did during practice. Joe, who had been the star quarterback, then later a fullback on the football team, was playing, and all of a sudden he went down with a broken leg.

During practice, if some of the starters finished a little early, the coach would let them go to the showers, and then he'd put the rest of us into the game. Of course, some of us hadn't been getting much practice, but when Joe went down, the rest of us all felt psychologically decimated—the starting guard was gone, and there was nobody to take his place. There was no guard to finish that night's practice.

The coach looked at me and said, "Bones, you can't play anything else. Come out here and play guard the rest of the night."

I said to myself, *What the heck? I'll probably get cut, so I'm just going to have some fun.* We were playing half-court, so every time the ball went to the basket, I just ran up and tipped it in. At about six feet, seven inches tall, I now weighed about 175 pounds. I was just playing like I did in the backyard with the guys, and I was having a good time.

We showered after practice, and the next night we were to go play Cyprus.

Some of the kids in our farming community went to Cyprus, and some to Granite, but we all knew each other, and we'd played basketball with each other in the stake that summer. One of those kids had gone to Granite his sophomore year, then transferred to Cyprus as a junior and made All-State. Still, I could beat him one-on-one in the backyard.

Coach Baker hadn't said anything about who would start at the other guard, though his son was a starting guard. I was kind of concerned because I knew that after this game, a list on the board on Monday would tell the four or five of us who would make the team and who would get cut. After warm-ups, Coach Baker said, "Bones, you're going to start at guard tonight."

But I'd never played guard, not even in church basketball, though in the yard, I'd played a little bit of every position.

I looked at the coach and didn't know what to say. A fear came over me. I hadn't even practiced with the starting team other than for a few minutes, and I didn't know what to do.

"Bones," the coach continued, "all I want you to do is get the rebounds, and then give the ball to Drestan or Mitchell. And I want you to stop Willardson from scoring."

That assignment didn't bother me—I'd played old Jay in the back yard and knew I could handle him.

"And by the way," the coach added, "you'll jump center."

Our center was Glenn Smith, who also stood at six feet, seven; and Marvin Eyre was just about the same height. Droston Baker, at six feet-two, played guard, and the other forward was Mitchell, the fastest guy on the team. We had tip-off plays, but again, I had never jumped center.

The coach explained the little signals we used on tip-offs. I got the tip-off, and Mitchell put the ball in the basket.

I played the entire game and held Jay to about four or five points. When I told my mom and dad that I had played the whole ballgame, they couldn't believe it.

I became the starting guard for the whole season and was never taken out of a ballgame except when I fouled out in the Ogden game. I wasn't a very good ball player—I couldn't shoot from the outside, though I was pretty quick and could block shots and get rebounds.

On the way to a game in Ogden, the coach took five of us aside and said, "Now Bones, I don't want you to do any shooting tonight. If you take a shot from outside the foul line, you'll sit on the bench for a whole quarter."

That was all right by me. I'd been averaging only about one or two shots a game anyway.

When we played Ogden High School, nobody was even guarding me. I just passed the ball around, usually to our center, so he could score. My main responsibility was to try to stop the fast break. We played what we called the Granite Zone Defense. (If I ever coached, that's the defense I'd teach. Though it's a tough defense to learn, it makes the other team think you're playing zone, when you're really playing man-to-man. It just takes an awful lot of practice.) The object was to not let the other team score, and when you got the ball, you played a kind of freeze-out. (We were averaging only about twenty-two points a game, and we still won the state championship.) Anyway, the quarter was just about over, and I cast up an eighteen- or twenty-foot shot, which didn't even hit the rim. Sure enough, my friend Reed, who had been on the team the year before, came in and replaced me.

So I sat on the bench. At the end of the quarter, the coach said to me, "You can go back in."

We lost that game by three or four points, something like 25 to 21.

On the way home, Coach Baker said to me, "Bones, we lost that game because you weren't in there."

I reminded him that he'd been the one who who'd taken me out.

"That's because you broke a rule. Now the next game, remember, you don't shoot."

So here we were playing ball games and my only scoring was a foul shot or a tip-in. And we didn't shoot any foul shots, because of the rules in those days. On any foul, you had the option of shooting the two foul shots or taking the ball out of bounds. We always took the ball out of bounds, because then you had the chance of a two-point basket. So I was averaging maybe one to three points a game, though in a couple of games I scored eight or ten points.

By now, we're playing in the state tournament, and Coach Baker never let us watch an opponent play. That just wasn't done in those days. As the season went along, East High School was leading the state in scoring and everything else. Jordan High school was also pretty good, as were Box Elder and Weber, up north.

East High had a big center, Willie, and a kid named Clark, who could really shoot the ball and was the leading scorer in the state, sometimes putting in thirty points in a ballgame. Our whole team was averaging only a few over twenty. So all week we practiced to play East High School in regionals, playing our zone defense, a little altered. The coach put me on Clark, and when the game was over, we'd won 26 to 21. Clark had scored only four points.

We beat Logan by four points, and then were set to play Weber High School in the state championships, and Weber had outstanding ball players. They had beaten Box Elder for the regional championship, so they went into the tournament seeded as number one. In the seeding, East, Jordan and Granite were in a three-way tie. We flipped for seeding. East drew the #1 seed, Jordan drew #2, and we drew #3. Now we had to play Logan, the best seed in the coach's eyes, though I disagreed with him. Number 1 seed was best in my judgment.

Weber won big the first night by about 20 points, so we had to play them. Things didn't go well for us at all the first half. Weber had about an 8- or 10-point lead, and we'd hardly ever had 23 points scored against us in a whole game. But Weber wasn't guarding me, only double-teaming Smith and sagging off on Mitchell, our two scorers. We just weren't putting the ball in the basket.

After two or three timeouts, we still didn't know what to do. When I got a rebound, I'd dribble down the court, then usually pass off to Baker or Mitchell, who ran the offense. Then I got the idea that I would play a little barnyard basketball—where the idea came from, I don't know. Over the years, I've liked to think I was inspired.

So I just took off, went right down the middle, and made a lay-up. Nobody even tried to stop me. The next time I came down the court, again nobody came to stop me. It's now two or three minutes before halftime, and Weber called a timeout. Coach Baker congratulated me for what I'd done—making two lay-ups.

So when we came back on the court, the coach said to me, "Bones, you can play pretty good. Why don't you start crashing the boards? We've held you back to stop the fast break, but now we need somebody who can get up on the boards, and we need to put some shots up. Our control game isn't working, and we've got to get some quicker shots and catch up."

Sure enough, Weber put in a guy to guard me in some kind of token defense. I just passed the ball to Glen, who handed it off to me as I went down the middle, and I got another lay-up. I scored eight points in the last two minutes of the first half, and we went to the locker room only four points down.

The last half, the coach gave me the same instructions: crash the boards. Weber made another adjustment, but now every time I was given the ball, Weber would double-team Mitchell, our driver, so I still wasn't being guarded very well. I got two tip-ins the second half.

We went on to beat Weber that night, scoring more points that night, 43, than we'd ever scored before. Glen got 12, Marvin 12, and I got 12.

The next night we were to play Box Elder, who had Don Malmrose, who could shoot the ball as well as anyone I have ever seen in high school or college. Talk about shoot! And he was the smoothest ball player I'd also ever seen. I still remember some of the names of some of the team. (One of them is still a friend of mine, and every time he sees me, he moans about that ball game, having relived it for fifty years.)

The night of the game, Coach Baker walked us out on the University of Utah football field, where he explained how he wanted us to play our defense. We adjusted our zone so that if Malmrose was playing out, I would take the place of Mitchell; and if the ball went to Malmrose, it was my responsibility to get on him so he couldn't shoot. I was pretty nervous about it all.

Sure enough, when the game started, Malmrose was on the right side, where he loved to shoot from. His first bucket went right in.

The next times he came down, I would sneak up on him, and he ended up with only four points for the whole ballgame.

It was a tight game, and it ended up in a 25-25 tie. Each of us on the team had five points, and we had all played the whole game—no substitutions. I had got my five points off two tip-ins and one foul shot.

Now it was overtime, in those days only three minutes long. If neither team was ahead at the end of overtime, then it was sudden-death—whoever scored first won the game. On any five-second violation, there was a jump ball (now the ball goes to the other team).

We had our tip-off plays, and we usually got the tip-off and scored the first points of the game. Sure enough, I got the tip-off, we ran our plan, and Mitchell got a lay-up and was fouled. He made the foul shot. Why the coach didn't have us take the ball out, I don't know, but at least we now had a three-point lead.

Our strategy was to pass me the ball. I'd hold it above my head, allow a tie ball, and then we'd jump and get the tip again.

Box Elder brought the ball down and threw it to Malmrose, and everyone just knew he was going to put in a basket, but I had been crowding him pretty close. As he faked to go around me, I stepped in front of him. When he saw my big, long arm come up, he threw the ball about ten feet over the hoop and out of bounds. (In that kind of excitement, that can happen to any kid.)

We now had the ball, passing it around in a kind of weave and stall, nothing sophisticated. Because I was not allowed to dribble, I'd just move to the corner, and pretty soon the ball would come to me. Then a guard would have to come to me, because they were pressing all of us, but now I'm not throwing the ball to anybody—"Jump ball!"

I'd get the tip, we'd pass the ball around, and pretty soon it would come back to me. I don't know how many jump balls we had, but time soon ran out, and we'd won 28 to 25, just by stalling. We'd never taken another shot.

And we did take the state championship.

The newspapers had selected me All-State the day before, something I'd never anticipated and the biggest surprise of my life. Reporters swarmed into the dressing room. A guy named Floyd Millet, a BYU basketball coach, walked up to me. He said he'd seen my first game against Cyprus, and had wondered how Coach Baker had got that kid out there playing for him. But he'd been watching me over the year: "I'd like to offer you a scholarship to play for BYU."

I looked at him, not even knowing who he was, and mumbled, "Well, thanks."

"We'll get in touch with you."

I didn't know what was going on.

On the way home from ballgames, the coach would usually take us to get a hamburger or eggnog-banana milkshake (with nutmeg) at a place called Cummings Drive-In on Main Street in Salt Lake City. So that night, we had a real celebration, not getting just a hamburger, but also the milkshake and a root beer to go with it all.

My dad was never one to go to any of the games, and neither was my mother. They weren't into sports like I was. On Monday, there was to be a championship celebration assembly at the high school, though I didn't know what that meant either. So I went dressed like I always did, and suddenly the team were asked to get up and give speeches. Talk about embarrassed—I could hardly say anything. I just stood there, terrified and shy. I have a picture of the scene, whose caption says, "Herschel Pedersen's shy."

The Lion's Club gave the team several dinners for winning the title for the community, and I started getting phone calls and letters from people wanting me to play college basketball. College? I'd never heard of such a thing. Glenn Smith, Marvin Eyre and I were being hustled all over by people wanting us to come and play ball for them.

Thanks to one of my teachers who knew I didn't have any money to go to college and so was looking out for me, I received one scholarship from Union Pacific Railroad and another from Future Farmers of America and Northrup-King Seed Company if I would go to Utah State. So I had an athletic scholarship and two other scholarships if I would play basketball and go into horticulture. I was tempted to accept them.

The three of us took a trip on a Greyhound bus to Utah State Agricultural College (now Utah State University), bus fare paid by the college. We were taken to the gymnasium, where quite a few guys invited us to come and play there on scholarship. We played a little with the varsity basketball team.

The last night, we were guests at a sorority-fraternity party, to get a taste of social life on campus. Now I had never been on a date, and neither had Glenn Smith, and here we were at a lousy party, drinking punch and standing around like a couple of idiots. Girls would come up to us and want to dance. (Marv Eyre was engaged to a girl at the time, though he did dance a bit.) Talk about an embarrassing mess—I was completely out of my element.

We slept in a college dorm, and two days later, we took the bus home. I commented to Glenn, "Well, I'm not going up there. That sorority party stuff is not for me."

I turned all these down and went to BYU. I think the Lord sent me there. BYU didn't even have its own gymnasium to play in, only a place on the third floor of the old Education Building where the team could practice. The Women's Gym, on University Avenue, could only seat about twenty people, so the team played their games in the old Springville High School gymnasium. The coach's office wasn't even as good as most high school coaches' offices.

Five of us from the high school visited BYU, thanks to ten dollars gas money given to someone to drive us down. All the buildings were old, except for the new Joseph Smith Building, and you had to walk several blocks from lower campus to upper campus. The tennis courts were out-of-doors. Part of the campus was an open field of sagebrush. BYU was the sorriest place you ever saw.

We went to dinner to a place in Springville called The Chicken Roof, but were told we couldn't spend more than $1.50 for the meal. In short, BYU didn't have any recruitment money.

In those days, you didn't sign a letter of intent; you only made a verbal commitment. Two of my buddies agreed to play football for BYU, and I agreed to play basketball. Glenn Smith said he wasn't going to go to school anywhere that year. He worked for a year at the Tooele Army Depot, then went to the University of Utah on a scholarship. (By that time I was on a mission in Denmark.) Marvin Eyre played professional baseball—he could throw a baseball so hard it looked like an aspirin coming at you.

I had talked to my mother and father about BYU: "Boy, this Church is really struggling. BYU has nothing down there." But some of the other athletes recruited to BYU were saying they wanted to build a team. And architects were already designing a field house, to be finished by the time I would graduate.

I also told my mom and dad, "I really want to be a farmer someday, or maybe a rancher, and those poor folks at BYU are not going to get anybody down there to play basketball."

I've been told I may have been the first person to attend BYU on an athletic scholarship, go on a mission, and then return to play. I was not a member of the national championship team, yet I was well known on campus and well thought of, even though as a student I did a lot of things I shouldn't have.

Chapter Three

Bones as a Nickname

How did I get to be called "Bones"? When I was a kid growing up, I was six foot, two inches tall in the ninth grade, and skinny as a rail. Richard Kevins started calling me "Soup Bone." That stuck with me all through high school. When I got to BYU, Coach started calling me just "Soup." Then he added, "No, there's not enough meat on your bones to be called 'Soup Bones.' We'll just limit it to 'Bones.'" That's how I became known as "Bones."

When Robert Matthews was called by Gordon B. Hinckley to be the president of the Mt. Timpanogos Temple, he was given a week or two to pick his counselors. I don't know how he came to choose me; all I know is that when he met with President Hinckley to turn in names, the president looked at them and asked, "Herschel Pedersen? Who's he?"

President Matthews said, "Bones."

"Oh, you means Bones Pedersen? Yes, we know him."

When President James E. Faust of the First Presidency spoke at a meeting that my wife and I attended, he looked down and said, "There's my friend Bones."

I'm known more by that name than my real name. It doesn't bother me at all. I find it quite nice to be called that.

<u>Chapter Four</u>

Freshman Basketball at BYU

Anyway, when I decided to go to BYU, the basketball team invited me to come to practice every Tuesday and Thursday in what was called "unofficial workouts." The assistant coach, Millet, would be there. (In those days, freshmen were not allowed to play varsity basketball.) Old Pinky H., from Las Vegas, was on the team, and he was the best passer I ever played with. (After two years, he was cut, but he later won conference in throwing the javelin in track and field.)

We ended up that fall with twelve of us on the freshman team, all of us All-Staters from somewhere.

At our first practice, while running drills, Coach Millet came up to me and said, "Bones, you can't even comb your hair with your left hand. Go down to the other end of the court and practice till you can do something with that left hand." He came down and showed me some things he wanted me to do. After half an hour practicing alone, he came back and said, "Now before you come back next week, I want you to do these things better."

So I went home and practiced these things in my backyard—things I'd never been taught. When the season came along, the announcement came that I would play center, because BYU already had a lot of guard recruits. We practiced and practiced.

Our first game was with Weber Junior College (Weber State College). Coach Stan Watts had plays, I knew them, and we ran them, but we were still losing. At the end of the first quarter, the coach (who had coached Jordan High School when I played at Granite High School) said to me, "Bones, I want you to go in and play guard. Do what you did in high school, and shut their shooter down."

So for the rest of the game, I played guard, though the next week I practiced both center and guard, playing both positions. Sometimes I'd start, and sometimes I wouldn't. Coach Watts had a way of rotating us all around, keeping us all happy. Everybody got to play, and everybody got to sit on the bench.

As the season came on, our freshman team was whipping everybody. About a month before the season was over, Coach Millet announced that he was going to have a couple of scrimmages between the freshmen team and the varsity, and this was going to be a game with real officials. Of course the Springville gym was sold out. (It didn't hold very many people anyway.) The newspaper reporters came down, and we beat the varsity by twelve points—this even though the varsity later in the season won the conference title!

When the season was over, I dropped out of school because I wanted to work and save some money. I was through playing ball. I was a poor kid, and I especially wanted to have my own car, and there might be something else I would want to do with my money someday. I'd had a good job working at the Wool Company in Salt Lake City ever since I was in the ninth grade, so I went back to work there, and I also got my friends jobs there. This is when I had one of the great spiritual experiences of my life.

An old forest ranger also worked there. At that time, there were martins in the Uintahs, and trapping permits were being issued. The pelts were made into sable coats, and those pelts were selling for about sixty to seventy dollars apiece. My friends and I got permits and bought traps and warm clothing. If I wasn't going to school that winter, I would make myself a thousand dollars trapping martins in the Uintahs.

Then it came time for me to be interviewed to go on a mission.

Herschel's photo for the 1955-1956 BYU game program.

MISSION CALL

One day my mother said to me, "Herschel, the stake president's comin' to see you tonight."

"Well, good. What time's he comin'?"

I was naked to the waist, I had a few cows to milk, and my buddies were there waitin' to go rabbit huntin' about six o'clock.

I was making $52 a week and spending half of it on shotgun or .22 shells. I considered myself the "great hunter" and I was the best shot in town.

But here comes the stake president, driving right up behind my buddy's car, so my buddy can't get his car out of the driveway. "What are you gonna do?" my buddies ask me.

"Oh, I believe he's goin' to ask me to go on a mission. I'll only be three minutes. I'll tell him I ain't goin'."

The stake president comes up to me and says, "I want to talk to you. Get in the back seat of my car."

This is all happening at the end of July, and stake conference is a couple of weeks away.

He rolls the window shut—I guess he doesn't want anybody listening to what we say. "I guess you know why I'm here," he says.

"Yeah, I think you came to talk to me about goin' on a mission."

"That's right. You ought to go on a mission. What do you think about that?"

"I don't know if I'm worthy or not."

"You'll have an interview with a General Authority, and he'll determine that. But would you go?"

I say, "I'll be glad to go." Then I take a look at myself and think, *What did I just say? I've just told my buddies I'd only be three minutes, because I was going to say I wasn't going on a mission.*

"Okay," the stake president says. "I'll schedule your interview when the General Authority comes to stake conference." In those days, a General Authority always visited the quarterly stake conferences, and everyone who went on a mission was interviewed by a General Authority. All the young men who were going on missions would line up for an interview.

As I walk out of the car, my parents ask me, "What did he want?"

"He wants me to go on a mission. You knew that."

"Yeah. What did you tell him?"

"I told him I'd go."

They look at me and don't say anything—not a thing!

When I get in the car with my buddies to go rabbit hunting, they ask me, "What did you tell him?"

I tell them what I told my parents.

"How come you said that?"

"I've got to keep my word. If I'm called, I guess I'll go."

What I didn't know till years later was that my grandmother, my uncles and my aunts all knew about the call, and they'd been fasting and praying, because they knew I didn't want to go on a mission. They'd even come to the house that evening while I was milking and had a prayer, asking the Lord to inspire me, compel me, or do whatever, to go on a mission.

The great thing about the story is that not until I came home from my mission did they tell me all this. Also, "The day you got in the backseat of that car, every one of us saw an angel—one on the left and one on the right. When you got in the car, they got in with you. That's why you said yes."

The way I grew up, these aunts and uncles and everybody else were preaching at me every day while I was hauling hay or doing other farm jobs. Sometimes they'd even get in arguments over Church doctrines. By the time I was ten years old, I'd heard more gospel preached than most people hear in a lifetime. I had even heard things discussed in the hayfield that we don't publicly talk about now.

I was the first one of the young men to be interviewed at stake conference by Brother LeGrand Richards, who at that time was the Presiding Bishop of the Church. I was really shaking. I knew that God was going to reveal to Brother Richards every bad thing I'd ever done wrong—every bad word I'd ever said, every bad thought I'd ever thought. I would never go on that mission, and my family were going to be disappointed.

My knuckles went white from gripping the arms of the chair. Brother Richards looked at me and asked, "So you want to go on a mission?"

"I didn't say that, Sir."

"Well, I've got a couple of papers here to sign, and then I'll ask you some questions."

He signed the papers and kind of pushed them to the side. "I need to ask you some more questions."

"Yes, sir."

"Are you morally clean?

Missionaries wore hats until the 1960s. This photo was taken for Herschel's mission to Denmark in 1948-1951.

"Sir, I can answer yes to that question."

"You look like you're a little nervous."

"Yes, sir, I *am* nervous."

"Then why don't you go home?"

"Yes, sir."

The interview was over and I walked out the door.

My friend who lived across the street from me, and who I thought was a lot better guy than I was, had a half-hour interview.

On the way home, my mother asked me, "What did Brother Richards say?"

I described the interview, then added, "So here I am, going home."

Now my mother began to worry about me.

Earlier that year, she had almost died, but then recovered. My father administered to her. She told him that the next time he administered to her, he would not be able to bring her back. She would be gone. At one point, while unconscious, she had visited the spirit world for three days, where she had some remarkable visions. She was promised that if she would do whatever God wanted her to do, her family would remain faithful in the Church all their lives. I thought she was a bit balmy, talking about the spirit world like that, telling me things we wouldn't even record in our journals—but it all ended up being true. About two weeks before she passed away, she told me that she was worried about me.

The fact was that I was supposed to return to play basketball at BYU. I was supposed to have gone down to register for fall quarter on a Friday, but I hadn't done it. My mother asked me, "Aren't you doing to play ball this year, and get your education?"

I confessed, "I really haven't been studying. I don't think I'm going to register."

My parents couldn't get me to go back to school, and the mission call hadn't come yet. Also, I had made other plans. I told my mother, "I'm going up in the hills and trap marlins"—whose pelts were going for about $75 apiece. My buddies and I had permits and had made arrangements to stay in a cabin. We figured we could come home with a couple of thousand dollars each. I had seventy-two traps, and I'd bought me some air force flying boots. Everything was ready to go.

Sunday was a cold, drizzly day. I was sitting in the house, doing nothing, when there was a knock on the door. I looked up, and there was Coach Watts, Wayne Soffe, and Eddie Kimball—the basketball coach, his assistant, and the director of athletics. Now I was really in trouble.

I'd told them in the spring that I would be back in the fall, and every Tuesday and Thursday night I'd gone to informal workouts with the basketball team.

So there we all were—me, my mother, my father, and those three guys from BYU. It was kind of like before a jury. In my mind, I wanted to go trapping marlins. I also really wanted to play basketball, and then there was the talk about me going on a mission, though I hadn't got a call. The BYU guys talked about how they needed me at BYU. My parents added, "You'd better go down." In fact, as I said, our freshman team had regularly beat the varsity team. We played all our games in the Springville High School gym, because BYU still didn't have a basketball gymnasium.

I looked at them all and said to the coaches, "I'm sorry. I should have been honest with you. I'm not gonna return to BYU. I'm going on a mission."

My mother and father looked at me. You see, it had been almost two months since I'd had my interview with Brother Richards. Then the thought just came to me: *I'll be going on a mission.* I knew right then that I'd be going.

"I know I don't have a call," I explained, "but I'll get one." (That kind of thing has happened to me many times in my life—I've known something that turned out to be exactly how I thought it would be.)

The coaches looked at me: "Good. We appreciate your decision. When you come home from your mission, you'll have a scholarship. But do write us a letter once in a while."

"You bet I will." And I did write Coach Watts. He'd send me clippings from the newspaper on how the "Y" was doing in basketball and tell me a little about team members.

Now I was trembling because I was a sinner. I'd been running around with a bunch of guys who were the worst poachers in the business. I could catch pheasants and fish with my bare hands. I hunted rabbits almost every day. I shot out streetlights. My attitude had been, *Heck, I'm not goin' on no mission.* My buddies and I had all agreed that we weren't going on no missions.

My brother, who'd been majoring in physics at the University of Utah, had stopped by for an interview by a General Authority and had his mission call in two weeks, but me, I was waiting. It was October and I was getting ready for the deer hunt. I'd been catching pheasants, feeding them in our chicken coop, and selling them to the rich people in Salt Lake City who wanted a pheasant dinner. (That gave me more money to buy shotgun shells.) I wasn't swearing or breaking the law too much, or doing anything else very wrong. And I was trying to repent of the things I'd done wrong.

About two days before deer season, I got a call to the Danish Mission, but I wasn't scheduled to leave till January.

When I finally got that call, a tragedy happened: My mother died on a Tuesday, we buried her on Thursday, and my farewell was on Sunday. Harold B. Lee, who had been our stake president and was now a member of the Quorum of the Twelve, spoke at Mother's funeral, and I was one of the pallbearers.

So by the time she passed away, I was having my missionary farewell. (She's appeared to some of my brothers and sisters since her death, though I myself haven't received a visitation.)

For my missionary farewell, the chapel was full of people. I was terrified. It was the same thing I'd experienced before basketball games in high school (when we'd won the state championship) and at BYU. I'd be so nervous before a game that I could hardly do anything until the game started. So here at the farewell, I'd have given anything to get out of the chapel.

The head of the Utah State Highway Patrol, and second counselor to the bishop (who was my uncle), was conducting the meeting. He stood up and said, "Brothers and sisters, there's been a little tragedy. Soup Bones' mother died, and we buried her last Thursday. We appreciate you all coming to his farewell. Why don't we present Herschel with the money that's been contributed to his mission?" (In those days, there was a table in the foyer where people could throw money for the missionary as they came to the farewell.)

I received enough money to take care of the first ten months of my two-and-a-half-year mission—something I'd never expected. I didn't think the people in the ward who knew I poached pheasants liked me very well. At least they never said anything about that to me. But they gave me all that money, and now I felt worse than ever. I looked at those people, put my head down, and fought the tears that came to my eyes. I got to thinking, *How could I have been such a rotten guy all these years?*

The officer went on: "You know, a lot of you people have called me and told me we ought to arrest Herschel Pedersen, because he's out poaching birds or doing somethin' else against the law. But this guy has got so good at what he does, he can catch a fish with his bare hands. And he caught all those pheasants with his bare hands—he didn't shoot any of them. Yes, he's got a coop full of 'em. When he leaves, we're going to turn them all loose. Anybody who's that skilled ought to be allowed to use his skill. So we've never put any pressure on him or arrested him."

He then asked my father to speak, but he choked up and couldn't hardly say anything because my mother had just passed away.

The agriculture teacher at Granite High School spoke, and so did my coach, about five minutes each. I'd been the state crop-judging champion for three years through the FFA and won the award for Outstanding Future Farmer. I'd also had grand champion pigs in the State of Utah for four years. I'd even been appointed Assistant Swine Director at the Utah State Fair—a paying job, fifty bucks for a week at the fair. Fifty bucks!

So everybody talked about all the things I'd done, and then the time was turned over to me. When I looked down at all those people, I was terrified—I'd never been so terrified in all my life. I said (and I've since memorized the speech), "Thanks for coming. Thanks for your money. God bless you. In the name of Jesus Christ, Amen." It was the shortest sacrament meeting ever held in that ward.

The officer got up and said, "Well, when Herschel comes home, I guarantee he'll have more to say."

I'd been in trouble all my life until I went in the mission field, and now people were telling me, "You could never have been that way." But if they had talked to a certain aunt, or to my brothers and sisters, they'd have told you that I had been a sinner and was certainly the shyest kid in town. What changed me is what happened in the mission field.

MY FIRST CONVERSION

I came from a poor family. Because World War II had just ended, and my brother had just come home from the army, three of us brothers were on two-and-a-half-year missions in Denmark at one time.

There was no missionary training center in the Church then like there is now. New missionaries went to the temple one day, were told a few things in the Beehive House, and then were set apart the next day. They left on the train the following day.

I left Salt Lake City in the winter of '49, one of the snowiest winters on record. The train got stalled somewhere out of Cheyenne, Wyoming and had to be plowed out. We missionaries sat on the train having fun talking about our high schools, who's going to which mission, and so on.

A Protestant minister on the train happened to come through our car and stopped right where I was sitting. He started to challenge our religion. I didn't know a lot, only two or three scriptures I'd learned in seminary or heard my parents and grandfather recite. I whipped out my Bible and started reading those scriptures. Did he ever twist them around! He's telling this dumb kid that scriptures mean this, they don't mean that. By the time we got to Chicago, that guy had me wondering if I knew what I was talking about. Even though I thought I had a testimony of the gospel when I left on my mission, it wasn't till I arrived in Denmark that it started to build.

We did get to New York City on time to catch our ship.

I happened to get a companion by the name of John D. Clawson from Seattle, Washington. My mission president told me, "I'm giving you a companion who is the best working missionary in the mission field."

My first day in Denmark, in Aarhus, the sixteen elders met at seven o'clock in the morning at the chapel. The first hour, we studied the Danish language under a Danish Sister who spoke good English. (She later married a returned missionary.) We had elders in the mission who had been in the military, and some had seen combat, but there were also elders just out of high school who had had one year of college. So when it came time to do missionary work, there was no playing, no goofing off. These older men—branch presidents, district presidents—were running the mission. They knew what misery was. One elder, about twenty-six years old, had been a prisoner of war. Another had been a paratrooper dropped in behind enemy lines, and he was wounded twenty-nine times before he hit the ground and spent the rest of the war in a German hospital. These men were grateful just to be alive.

Missionaries held most of the leadership positions; all Danish leaders had been released after World War II because they needed to be retrained.

The first day out, Elder Clawson said to me, "I'll show you how it's done. The next door is yours." I thought he was joking. He rang the doorbell and a lady opened the door. Elder Clawson pushed me forward, saying, "Go ahead."

Talk about fear—I knew right then and there that I was ready to go home. But that's how the whole day went. Elder Clawson would push me forward, and then between doors, he'd try to teach me a few words to say.

The next day, I'm not trying to memorize scriptures, I'm trying to memorize some sentences to say at the door, because I was at the doors six hours a day.

Elder Clawson and I were up at five o'clock every morning, because we had to memorize our scriptures every day in Danish. But I mutilated my scripture, so that when I tried to pass it with the sister, she had to correct my pronunciation and everything. Between memorizing them in English and trying to memorize them in Danish, it was misery.

Then Elder Anderson would present some type of missionary thing, and Elder Clawson and I would go out and tract till noon. After a thirty-minute break for lunch, it was out tracting till 3:30—and this was every day. Each pair of elders was assigned a certain area of the city, so about every three weeks or so, we were knocking on the same doors—being told where we could go and how to get there.

Elder Clawson made me take every other door, and I couldn't even speak the language. And I was homesick! *This ain't fun,* I told myself. When I did start to understand the language a little, I concluded what I'd suspected on the train: The Lutherans twisted around all the scriptures which I believed proved the Church to be true.

This is no good, I said to myself. *I'm not doing any good here. I'm not doing my family or the Church any good. I ought to be sent home—but if I go home, I'll go home in disgrace.* I'd been in the mission field about a month and a half by then.

So I devised a plan: *I'll get up at five o'clock every morning and read the scriptures. I'll start with the Book of Mormon.* It was a rule to get up at 5:30 anyway and memorize scriptures in Danish. Then we had to pass those scriptures with that Danish sister who was trying to correct my pronunciation. It was pure misery.

I'll do every bit of my missionary work. I won't complain. When I finish the Book of Mormon, if I don't have a testimony, I'll at least know that I've given it all a fair shot. If the Book of Mormon is not true, I'll go home. If it's true, I'll be the hardest working missionary in Denmark, and I'll also be the happiest missionary in Denmark.

I read in the mornings. I read in the evenings. I read every chance I got. I kept praying. I kept fasting. I worked hard. My companion,

Elder Clawson, had the reputation for being the best working missionary in the mission (what a blessing!), and he was also in the branch presidency.

One day my companion announced, "I have to go across the road to the talk to Elder Christensen. You stay here. Lock the door and study. Make sure you see me enter the other missionaries' apartment."

I don't remember how long my companion was gone. I had just finished reading the Book of Mormon and was up to Section 9 of the Doctrine and Covenants. I knelt in prayer and told the Lord, "I've finished the Book of Mormon. I know I'm a sinner—I've done a lot of things wrong and maybe wasn't as worthy as I should have been to go on a mission. But you called me anyway, and here I am."

We missionaries had had an unusual experience in the mission home. The first morning we were there, a member of the Quorum of the Twelve stood before us in the Beehive House and just stared at us, not saying anything. By the time he was ready to talk, all the missionaries were staring right back at him. He said, "You are a sorry looking lot."

Denmark Mission photo, 1948-1951. This building is now the Copenhagen Denmark temple.

That struck me right in the heart.

He continued, "But if this is the best the Lord's got, I guess He'll just have to use you."

My attitude ever since has been, "Yes, I'm a sorry looking piece of humanity, but I'm the best the Lord has got, so He'll just have to use me."

I continued my prayer in Denmark: "Lord, we've been told we missionaries are a sorry lookin' bunch, but you're going to have to use us. I haven't been much good to you, but if the Church is true, I'll try to be a better person."

When I finished praying, I had an experience whose details I've never related and probably never will. I'll only say that the next day, when we went out tracting, I was no longer the same kid.

I will say that it was a profound spiritual experience of a very sacred nature. I can say that I know the Book of Mormon is true in ways that most people can only dream of. I'll only add that I've been very blessed since that experience. Whatever I've done in the Church has been a blessing to me, and whatever I've done outside the Church hasn't been as good. I had a very real experience.

Nobody can become converted unless they have a significant emotional and spiritual experience. That's the way it has to be. Alma asks, "Can you look up, having the image of God engraven upon your countenances" (Alma 5:19). This means that your testimony should be carved in your heart, as if it were on stone or metal.

At doors, my Danish was now clear, and I had something to tell the people. I was getting invited into houses—all this because there was a difference in me. I never had another sad day in the mission field. The change that took place in me that day in Denmark has been with me ever since. Anytime something goes wrong and I feel like murmuring or complaining, I think back to that day. In fact, fifty years later, I took my wife back to that apartment and took a picture of it: Number 10, Tennegade, Aarhus, Denmark.

So my childhood fears of speaking in public changed in Denmark. After the war, it was mainly missionaries who spoke in church meetings, so you had to speak almost every week. If you were in a small branch, you were a member of the branch presidency. When Earl Clark and I were sent to Bonholm, there were no members, so we had to do the singing, the preaching, and the teaching. One of us would give the opening prayer, and the other the closing prayer.

Also, there were no missionary lessons like there are now—you could teach anything you wanted. We didn't even have copies of the Book of Mormon to give to the Danish people. A missionary's calling was simply, "Go out and teach."

Whenever or wherever we taught, whatever came out, came out. We did what the scriptures said to do: Take no thought of what you are going to say.

Elder Anderson and his companion would do all the talking at the doors, and his companion, Elder Clark, would let him do it. So after a few months, I spoke better Danish than Elder Clark did. Then Elder Anderson, who was the supervising elder in the district, asked me and his companion to work together in a certain part of the city on our own on Tuesdays and Thursdays.

The first day this elder and I went out, he would get to stuttering and couldn't say anything. I ended up doing about eighty-five percent of the talking. By now, I was speaking better Danish than some missionaries who had been there two years—just because of those experiences with Elder Clawson. And somehow I had learned that getting in a door was a challenge. Even if people tell you they're not interested, you find a way to get in.

Brother Clawson and I still communicate. He has retired and now lives in Florida. I even performed a marriage for his granddaughter at the Mt. Timpanogos Temple. The thing is, if it hadn't been for him forcing me to speak Danish (and it was pure agony), what kind of a missionary would I have been? During the last part of my mission, I loved to tract—it was my favorite thing. When I got a new missionary, I did the same thing to him: "Hey, we're going out today, and we're going to have a great day. Here's a house we haven't gotten into for fifteen weeks."

We'd been out about seven months when we met a professor from the University of Aarhus. As missionaries we had been to his home probably a dozen times, and one day he told me to go to hell—he was not interested. But this morning we had prayed that we would be able to get in and talk to this man.

We had a little typewritten tract titled "We Present Ourselves," which we always offered this man, though he wouldn't take it. So this day my companion and I each folded a twenty-dollar bill in the tract (I was only getting $35.00 a month).

When we knocked on his door, he said, "Are you guys back again?"—that kind of an attitude. "Look, I know you're Americans, and I know you're from the Mormon Church, but I'm not interested in religion of any kind. I teach anthropology at the university, and that six-day creation thing in the Bible is a bunch of junk."

We answered, "Look, we've been coming all these times. You ought to let us at least talk to you one time." Then we presented him the tract with the money in it, adding, "You might find something of value in it."

He opened it up, and there were two twenty-dollar bills, which at that time had a Danish exchange rate of about 6.50 or 7.00 Danish krone to the dollar.

When he realized they were dollars, he said, "Well, if you want to come in that bad, come on in."

We went in but didn't end up giving him the twenty dollars. After talking for a while, he said, "You know, I have a daughter who's just starting at the university. She might be interested in talking to you guys. She's not here today, but why don't you come back?

"And school's starting up in the fall. Why don't you come and see me once in a while, or come up and talk to my anthropology class. You can tell them your view of the creation or whatever you want."

This daughter wasn't interested, but she had a bunch of girlfriends in the area. When they saw us on the streets, they'd stop and talk to us. The daughter didn't start coming to church, but some of the other girls started showing up on their own. One of them joined the Church. At one time, she was the head Danish translator for the Church.

I was in Aarhus for eleven months, and all that group of young people eventually joined the Church.

DANISH BASKETBALL

The missionaries would tract from nine o'clock till lunch time, then tract again from one till about four, have supper, then work until about 10:30 at night. We had no time to prepare lessons, except early in the mornings.

We worked up to 120 hours a week, including study and meetings. I'd just get up in the morning and pray, "Lord, what do you want me to talk about this morning?" Then I'd open my scriptures to where I'd been reading, or open a Church book, and whatever I read, that's what I'd start teaching. I was blessed with the ability to remember what I'd read. And I've done that ever since.

After I'd been in the mission field about ten months, a letter from the mission president asked if any of the missionaries with basketball experience would like to play on a Danish team. Denmark was then trying to form a basketball Olympic team. The mission president had allowed a mission basketball team to practice just two hours a week on preparation day, so the team were all transferred to Copenhagen in late October. My companion, Gary Bjarnson, a six-foot, seven-inch ball player, had played for Springville High School; Darwin Larsen, an older elder who'd been in the military, also played with us, and he became our coach. We practiced a couple of hours on Saturday, then usually played a game the following Friday. Our team went undefeated, so when the season was over, we played the best team in Denmark and won the national championship game 82 to 7!

That's when the mission president gave permission for a couple of missionaries to teach the Danes basketball.

I sent my name in to play with the Olympic team and was selected. An active member of the Church in our branch, Willie Moritzen, also wanted to play basketball, though he was already a great soccer player, so he was fast. He became the starting guard on Denmark's Olympic team, though that team never scored more than 25 points or won a game because it was their first run. But that's how Denmark got its basketball team, and after that, a semiprofessional league developed in the country.

The next winter, my companion and I were assigned to go to the Danish basketball practices a couple of days a week, from three o'clock to five o'clock.

I'd been on my mission eleven months, and was now playing basketball, when President Sorensen called me to be the district president in Copenhagen, the largest district in Denmark. "We're having a district conference on Sunday. Brother Rasmussen, the district president, is being released, because he's immigrating to America." At that time, a district president was also the supervising elder, what we now call a zone leader. Thus I supervised all the elders in the Copenhagen District. Every morning from seven to nine o'clock, five days a week, all twenty-eight missionaries met in the chapel The first hour, I gave a lesson; and the second hour, we studied the language. My responsibility was to teach them how to do missionary work.

I said, "What?!" My thought was, *I can't do that.* The president also asked me not to say anything to my companion.

Right then, I started a three-day fast. My companion would ask me, "What are you fasting for?"

I'd tell him, "I'm in trouble. The mission president has talked to me, and I'm in bad trouble. I want outta here."

I was sustained on Sunday, and I was just terrified. First of all, I now had more responsibility. When we went to conferences in branches, we couldn't afford to ride the train, so my companion and I would bicycle—as many as ninety kilometers (about sixty miles). But we enjoyed it.

Because of this calling, my whole personality changed. I was often invited to speak at meetings and at firesides. As I look back, I see it as a great opportunity, but at the time, it was something of an embarrassment. It no longer bothered me to go up to anyone and talk to them about the Church. But even today, if you asked me to sell insurance, I'd be practically a dead man.

I also prepared lessons for the missionaries each morning, on topics of my own choosing. We had wonderful, spiritual experiences together for the fifteen months I was in Copenhagen. I also became involved in the missionaries' personal problems, activities that greatly helped me mature and prepare to accept later Church assignments on my mission and in my life.

At the time, we were celebrating the centennial of missionaries serving in Denmark. All missionaries were sent songs to practice—our mission president was a musician. Such wonderful songs as "I See a Holy Angel Flying" and "Hark, All Ye Nations" were translated into Danish, and we practiced for about fifteen minutes every morning at seven o'clock.

One of our missionaries, a dairy farmer boy from Plain City, Utah, was a good missionary. He could work the socks off just about any other missionary, and we became good friends. His junior companion was a handsome fellow from the Rexburg, Idaho area, and they weren't getting along very well, though both were good men. Every time the Rexburg missionary came to church meetings, all the Danish girls flocked around him like boys would to an ice cream freezer. (After World War II, the Danish girls outnumbered the Danish boys, and every girl felt it would be heaven if she could catch a missionary and come to the United States.) But the mission president always lectured the missionaries, "Don't get involved with the girls!"

Deseret News Drawing by Ev Thorpe, 1955

Still, even though this elder had a girlfriend back home waiting for him, he enjoyed the female attention. I had some talks with him about it.

The "girl problem" became an issue between the two missionaries. Add to that the fact that the junior companion had been in the mission more than six months but still had not learned to speak the language very well. Our companions were both teachers in the Primary, so I began to take this elder tracting with me during the two-hour Primary meeting. We became good friends.

Then one day he announced to me that he wanted to go home—and he was going to go tell the mission president. "My companion is a wonderful man, and he works hard, but he's always on me about the girls I attract and about other things. I know a lot of it is my fault, so I've got to have a transfer or else I'm going home."

I counseled him to just "hang in there. Pray about it. If you are transferred, where do you want to go?"

He wanted to stay in Copenhagen, adding that he wanted to become my companion, an arrangement that wouldn't be appropriate to propose to the mission president.

"Another thing," he said, "I don't have a testimony."

"You've gone to church since you were a kid! You've now been in the mission seven months. You *ought* to have a testimony. Have you read the Book of Mormon?"

"I still don't have a testimony," he insisted.

"I'll tell you what. You and I are going to start a little program." All my life I'd believed that these challenges are a matter of faith. I was able to get in the doors of people who didn't want to let us in, just by asking, "Lord, are we going to get in doors today?" I told my companion,

"Elder, we are going to set up a three-week program. You have nearly two and a half years left on your mission, and we don't have that much time to solve your problems. Besides that, I will have gone home before you do. So if you're going to be my companion and you want a testimony, we'll need to set up this three-week program for you. We're going to fast every Wednesday, but not tell our companions. We're going to do our regular missionary work, and if, at the end of three weeks, you haven't got a testimony, and President Sorensen doesn't call you to be my companion, then you can go home—and I'll go home with you."

"You can't do that!"

"I'd be glad to. God has never failed anybody. It says in the Good Book that if you pray in faith for something you need, you'll get it. You tell the Lord you need a testimony, and you want to be my companion for a while. If those things don't happen, then we'll both go home."

The elder felt that agreement to be a good one. For three weeks, we fasted one day a week, and I prayed that he would gain a testimony, but I wasn't praying about him becoming my companion. That wasn't my worry.

The last week, when our companions were busy in the Primary, we met in the chapel. He confessed, "I don't have a testimony, and I haven't been assigned as your companion."

I told him, "We still have twenty-four hours. Don't you worry. The Lord will take care of it."

"How can you be so sure?"

"I just know, just like I've known a lot of things, like that I was supposed to go on a mission. Who do you have faith in?"

"Well, I have faith in you."

"That's what it says in Alma 32:26: if you can no more than *desire* to believe in what I say, you'll have faith. I've been in the mission longer than you have, and I myself had bad times the first few months. I'd knock on doors but couldn't speak the language. But look at me today. I love being here, and tomorrow, you will love it too. Now let's go home and have a prayer and a good night's sleep."

At seven the next morning, after praying all night and while I was starting to teach my class, this elder came in, and he didn't look very happy at all.

About fifteen minutes into my hour-long lesson, President Sorensen opened the door. "Elder Pedersen, I don't want to interrupt you, but I need to see you and Elder So-and-so in the office as soon as this meeting is over."

We later went to his office, and as we walked in, he said,

"I don't know what's going on, but for three weeks, I've been observing you two missionaries, and you have been bothering me. I didn't sleep well last night because of you two young men. Elder Pedersen, you are my district president, and a good one. You've done everything I've told you to do. All the missionaries in the district are working harder and everything is going better.

"I've made a firm decision this morning, which will take effect today, whether you like it or not. Elder, you are to go to your apartment and pack your bags. You're to become Elder Pedersen's companion. Elder Pedersen's companion will become Elder Hancock's companion as of today. You two leave and have Elder Hancock come in.

"Didn't I tell you everything would be all right?" I said to him. "The Lord never lets you down, even though He sometimes comes through only at the last moment. That's the way faith operates."

Within three weeks, this elder was speaking Danish as well as I was. He hadn't been able to learn Danish because he'd been letting little things irritate him.

Even when I later worked at Geneva Steel, I was terrified when I had to correct people. I didn't like to do those kinds of things, even though I was in a position of leadership from the first day I worked there. I didn't know one man under me, though I soon learned to do pretty well at work. I got lots of honors and recognitions and came to be well respected. In the mission field, I taught the gospel, because that was my belief and commitment. I learned how to knock on doors and say, "We're going to get in."

We'd often been to the same door eight or ten times, so we'd heard every response one might give. We'd pray, then say, "We'll try something different." Doing that changed my personality—I became a somewhat different person.

One night when my companion and I were coming home late in a trolley car from some district meetings, we passed right by the chapel, where we had our bicycles parked. It was about ten o'clock at night, and we were supposed to be home at 9:30. We still had to get our bikes and ride on home. But here were a bunch of girls standing around, waiting to catch the trolley.

They flocked around my companion, saying, "Oh, Elder, it's so good to see you. We missed you at church tonight."

I looked at him, then at the girls, and said to them, "This elder is off limits. If I catch you talking to him again, I will see that he's transferred to the remotest part of the mission."

He looked at me. The girls looked at me. But the girls didn't talk to him anymore. I counseled him that he had to control such situations. "When someone comes up to you and says, 'Oh, it's good to see you,' you should say, 'Sister, my name is Elder So-and-so.'" That's what he did, and he never had any trouble with the sisters again.

HOMECOMING

I arrived at the railroad station at ten in the morning. My father met me and said, "Welcome home. We have supported you in the mission field as best we could, but you have three brothers still on missions. Don't expect any more financial help from us to go to school, or do whatever. God bless you, nevertheless. Let's go home. We've planned a little party for you."

We had a little weenie roast, and ate some watermelon and homemade ice cream. Aunts, uncles and others came to the party.

My draft notice was in the mail at eleven o'clock. The arrangement had been that I would write the draft board every six months for an extension of my deferment, and then notify them that I would be home on such and such a day. And that's the day I got my draft notice. The Korean War was on.

I had many good experiences in the mission field, but now I had come home, and there was a crowd at my homecoming, even though it hadn't been announced—nothing in the newspapers, no pictures, nothing. That's the way it should be, the way it is in the Church: you just go if you're asked to go, and you just come home when your mission is over. But here were my uncle, all these other good people, and my buddies from high school—all those people I thought I had offended by poaching pheasants and other game. Of course my father was also on the stand. The crowd was as big as it was when I had my farewell.

My mind reverted to how I felt at that farewell, and again, I began to withdraw within myself. Still I got up to the pulpit and said,

"I want to apologize to you for the short speech I gave when I left on my mission. Most of you know me. When I was around my friends, I was quite open, but before a crowd, especially to give a speech, I could hardly say anything. You all remember how we celebrated when the high school won the state basketball championship, and we all had to stand in front of the crowd. I was so embarrassed I couldn't say anything.

"I've just come back from two and a half years in the mission field, and I've been through a repentance process. I'm no longer the same man I was when I left. There will be no more breaking of the laws, no more doing the things I did that were wrong. I've learned something I want you people to know, something that will never let me down.

"When I went in the mission field, I thought I had a testimony because everyone in my family went to church. My father has been the bishop of this ward, as have my uncles. Everybody goes to church; if people are not in church, then something is wrong—you are sick, you have a broken leg, or the cows have gotten out.

"As I say, I now have a real testimony, which I gained in Denmark. Because of that testimony, I am now a responsible person. Like Joseph Smith, who knew what he knew and couldn't deny it, I know that God lives."

My speech lasted for about forty minutes, and after the meeting, the people all came forward and thanked me for it. They said they knew I had always had it in me—or something like that.

Chapter Five

Army Basketball

I was writing to the BYU coaches every six months, and they were replying that my scholarship was still good. But as soon as I got home from my mission, I was drafted into the army. The BYU coaches couldn't do anything about that, though they did offer me my scholarship when I returned from military service. I even worked out with the BYU team three or four times during the thirty days before I had to report to the army.

One day while I was in the army at Fort Ord, a bulletin was posted: there were going to be tryouts for the post basketball team, and if a man had played any college ball, he was invited to try out for the team. When I reported for tryouts, I couldn't believe how many men were there, but I ended up making the army basketball team, playing third-string center.

The guys ahead of me were Sabey, who had played for Fresno State, and a fellow by the name of Carter, a big black kid who had played for the University of California—and he was a good basketball player.

Playing volleyball for the Army in Otsu, Japan, 1952.

So now I'm traveling up and down the Pacific Coast, playing three or four ball games a week. College teams where then limited to a twenty-six-game schedule, but because of the Korean War, a military team could schedule practice games with them, and then the colleges didn't break any rules. So with nine All-Americans on our team, we're playing junior colleges and major colleges and universities, whipping them, and I'm getting to play three or four minutes a game.

There was a little dissension on our team—you can't put together a team of players from so many different systems. One day, an All-American from the University of San Francisco came up to me and asked, "How would you like to be the starting center on this team?"

"Frank, I'd love that. But I don't think it's a possibility."

"I'll fix that."

"How?"

"I have a favorite play. When I was playing for San Francisco, I'd come down the floor, I'd pass the ball to someone, he'd give it back to me, and I'd put it in the hoop. I know that's not one of the plays our coach has, but I'm an All-American, so he'll let me do just about whatever I want. If I score, he's not going to say anything. When you're in for your few minutes, you do that."

So the next couple of games, I gave him the ball.

Pretty soon, the little All-American guard from the University of Miami, Ohio, came up to me: "I'm got a little favorite play. I like to work a little jump shot over here. So when you're in the game, get me the ball."

Two weeks went by, and we're about to play the University of San Francisco. One of their players, an All-American, was averaging about 26 points a game. So these two players on my team said to me, "We've told the coach that you can stop him better than the two guys who are playing in front of you."

Now the guys are working with me in practice to get me ready to play the University of San Francisco.

I got to start that game, and of course that ticked off our starting center. I didn't say anything. I wasn't going to cause any trouble.

That night, I got the jump and played almost the whole game. We held San Francisco's star to fewer than ten points. I got twenty-four rebounds and became the starting center the rest of my time in the military—not to score, just to pass the ball to the others.

After playing basketball on the Coast, I was sent to Korea to fight in the Korean War. We went first to Japan, where we traveled by train, stopping in the City of Otsu, where we spent the night. As we were walking to the post exchange, a man by the name of Jim Acus approached us and asked if we were basketball players. Seeing that we were tall, he wondered about basketball. We told him that we had won the basketball championship in Camp Roberts the year before.

We went to the post library to find a copy of the *Stars & Stripes*, where an article reported our winning the championship. He called Major Julian Phillips. The next morning, as we were to leave for Sasebo, Japan, we were called out of line. Major Phillips told us that the U.S. Marine Corps had defeated the U.S. Army in basketball the week before. If we could beat the Marines on Friday night, none of us would have to go to Korea.

We defeated the Marine Corps, and I remained in Otsu on the basketball and volleyball teams.

I became the most valuable player in all the tournaments that we played in the army. Major Phillips told me that I was the only Mormon missionary he had ever met, but if he ever met another one, he would never have to serve in combat.

We played in the all-service tournament in Gifu, Japan. Everyone drank and chased the Japanese girls, while I went back to the barracks and read the Book of Mormon. I was considered a misfit for doing so.

Some years later, I was sitting in a stake priesthood meeting in American Fork. President Gene Priday, the stake president, asked the first BYU volleyball coach to come speak and tell about his conversion. The coach said he had been converted to the Church in Japan in the city of Gifu, where a Mormon missionary had played on the volleyball team for Otsu. And when the game was over, this young man would go back to the barracks and read the Book of Mormon. I asked myself, he continued, *What kind of man is this that would do this just because he didn't fit in?* So I went to the barracks and asked him what he was reading. I obtained a Book of Mormon, read it, joined the Church, and ended up being the first BYU volleyball coach.

He did not know that the missionary was in the audience he was speaking to.

I learned more about basketball through playing in the army than I ever learned anywhere else. We lost a couple of games, but now we were playing against a lot of teams with professional players. Our last year, we won the All-Army Championship in Japan, as well as the All-Service Championship.

By the time I finally returned to BYU, I'd spent two and a half years in the mission field and two years in the army. So I wasn't eligible to play until the end of the first quarter at BYU. In practices, I played third team, behind Blaine Anderson.

Chapter Six

Courtship and Marriage

Back at BYU, after my mission and the army, the team would practice basketball, then go to the food line at the Cougareat in the Joseph Smith Building—just like I had done in the army.

Way back when I was a senior in high school, a girl would come out to the farm and stand and talk to me while I was milking the cows. She once asked me to go on a date with six or eight of us, so we went to the movie *For Whom the Bell Tolls*. We were home by 10:30, and that was my only date till I went on another one five or six years later at BYU.

It was the mission that got me over my shyness, but on campus, I was still a social misfit because I never dated. I could preach the gospel, but I just couldn't ask a girl for a date. Janie Thompson, of the BYU Student Program Bureau, did persuade me and Bran Ranstrom, to be in a Negro minstrel show (before such shows were outlawed). We would do little dances and tell jokes in front of the curtain while the scenery behind the curtains was being changed. I also learned to do a little ballet routine before the student body, in which I played Cupid. Pictures were taken, which were in all the newspapers, including the *Provo Herald*. During a winter festival on campus, because of my reputation, a group made a snow sculpture of me about fifteen or twenty feet high. I was so popular that I was selected as one of the twelve outstanding students every year I was on campus, even though I thought I was outstanding in only one way—as a social misfit.

Here's how socially misfit I was. I was living with a couple of my brothers and some other guys. One of my brothers was dating all the time, and he'd proposed to two or three girls, only to be turned down. I myself was getting old by now—twenty-five. I prayed and said, "Lord, I haven't been doing any dating, and I ought to be married before I graduate, or my chances of finding a good wife won't be very good at all."

BYU then had Preference Balls, girls' choice. But I was never "chosen," though some of the girls in my geometry class did invite me to dinner. Shirley Falslev, the girl I later married, lived above them, though I didn't know it at the time.

Richard Horsley, the backup center on the basketball team, and I had become pretty good friends, even though we were quite different. We were both sometimes invited to this dinner, and it pretty soon became evident that everybody was trying to set me up with a girl in the apartment (my brother later married one of the girls in that apartment).

Six girls lived in the apartment. I didn't call the dinners a "date," just an invitation to dinner. Then one night Dick Horsley and some other guys who had been going to dinner announced that they hadn't been invited. *What's going on?* I asked myself.

Lo and behold, I was the only guy there—with these six girls! They asked me, "Why don't you take this girl out to the movie tonight?"

I'm thinking, *This isn't what I wanted.* I'd always been trying to get out of going to the girls' place alone.

"I'll tell you what," I finally said. "Why don't we *all* go down to the Paramount Theater?"

I loaded up all six girls in my little car and we went downtown. "I'd like to buy seven tickets to *Les Miserables,*" I told the girl at the ticket window. "This is a Brigham Young date, and I've got six girls with me tonight."

The girl looked at me rather strangely, and that was the last time I ever saw that bunch (though as I said, one of the girls later married my brother).

Once in a while when the basketball team were eating at the training table , one of the girls serving would come over and ask us if we wanted a glass of water, or another glass of milk, which they'd bring to us. The players would kind of flirt with some of the girls, and I did too. Because I'd never been on dates, the guys kind of heckled me about it, saying I didn't have the guts to ask a girl for a date.

One night at dinner, I said to the guys, "The next girl that comes to our table, I'll take her out."

A girl I didn't know from Adam came to the table and asked if we would like more water. I'd seen her in the line, but I didn't know her name. I said to her, "How would you like to go on a date?"

Her face flushed red.

"I'm serious," I continued. "I'm going to take you out on a date. These guys here say I can't get a date with a girl, so here's a sheet of paper. Write your name, address, and phone number on it. Tell me how to get to your house. The guys say we're going to a movie on Thursday."

Her face still red, she started to walk away.

"Hey, don't just walk away."

She finally agreed to go with me, though I think I embarrassed her more than I impressed her. But she was my second date.

One day in the Joseph Smith Building about one o'clock in the afternoon, on my way to get a milkshake before practice (hoping to put some more weight on my bones), I saw an old missionary acquaintance, Ray Madsen. We talked. He was waiting for his fiancé, a girl I'd known in my old Poplar Grove Ward. In a few minutes, she came by with another girl, and both were all smiles. The other girl was dressed in a blue skirt, a scarf around her neck, saddle shoes and "bobby socks," popular in those days. I was introduced, then went on my way for my milkshake. When she was introduced to me, I thought to myself, *There's a girl who enjoys life.*

As I said my prayers that evening, I realized I could not remember the girl's name. I told the Lord that I was indeed a misfit, but I needed to get married to a good girl. I had met a good girl that day, a girl with a beautiful smile. I told Him how she was dressed, but I couldn't remember her name. I also said I wanted a wife who was, first, virtuous; second, a good cook; and third, a woman I hoped also wanted twelve children. Fourth, she would have to understand my odd ways, and fifth, she would support me in whatever Church callings I received.

I added that whatever faults she might have, I would marry her if He would help me. I said nothing about me loving her, or her loving me. I thought that love would come. Of course I didn't love this girl—I'd just met her.

Playing basketball for the Camp Otsu Japan Green Waves during Army service 1952-53. Herschel was the tallest player and Stuki was the shortest.

I prayed about it, but I did nothing about it.

A couple of weeks later, I happened to bump into my missionary acquaintance again. He invited me to another missionary's home to see some slides from Denmark. But he said I should get a date—even though he knew I had not been on a date in years, and that no one would care to go with me. Still, he proposed that I take his fiancée's roommate—who happened to be Shirley. "She'll go," he insisted.

"I really don't want to go," I said—this after praying about Shirley every day.

Ray's girlfriend, Iris, agreed to ask Shirley if she would go with me. That was my first date with my future wife.

My brother was dating a girl from the apartment whose girls I had taken to the movie, and this girl's sister lived in Shirley's apartment. I hoped that the girls would talk and maybe tell me what Shirley had said.

Let me digress a bit. I had left the army with all sorts of awards, and also some jackets. But none of the jackets fit me. I was not only a social misfit, I was also a physical misfit. My arms and legs are proportionally longer than those of a normal person. But that didn't bother me, because I never worried about how I looked. I even wore logger boots to school, and clothes that didn't match. My green and yellow "Most Valuable Player" jacket, given me after an army tournament, was kind of warm, and even though it didn't fit me, I wore it anyway.

One day I was walking from a devotional at the field house up the steps to the science building with some of the basketball team. We were laughing, joking, as always, having fun. I'd lost some teeth in a ballgame and my eyes were black and blue and swollen. A couple of girls saw us, and one of them said, pointing to me, "Look at that! That's the ugliest thing I've ever seen in my life." (After we were engaged, Shirley told me she was the one who had said it.)

My sister Remore was taking a sociology class from a Dr. Woodruff. About two months into the school quarter, the professor was lecturing about people being socially out of place. For example, he told the class that Herschel Pedersen was the most socially misfit person on campus.

My sister told me what he'd said, so I got the time and place of the class, then dressed up in old logger boots, Levis and an old sweater from my mission days. I walked into the class about five minutes after the class started, sat down on the front row, and put my feet up on the desk. The class became completely silent, and the poor professor just looked at me.

"I hear you said I was the biggest misfit on campus, so I've come to hear it myself."

He apologized, but I told him there was no need for an apology. I knew I was different in many ways. We became friends.

Not long after this incident, I accompanied a missionary and his wife to a movie. I asked Shirley if she would go to the Danish Mission reunion about ten days later. To my surprise, she said yes. Another two weeks later, I called Shirley and asked her for another date. She accepted. Only this time, I would take her alone.

By now, I was getting courageous. I bumped into Shirley on campus a couple of days later and asked her on a date on my own. She said she'd go. I didn't tell her where we were going.

I picked her up about seven o'clock in the evening, and it was a freezing cold night. We drove up Provo Canyon to Bridal Veil Falls. Talk about a social misfit! (We laugh about it now, but it was no laughing matter then.) There was ice all over the parking lot.

I said to her, "Get out and get in the back seat."

She looked at me, fear in her eyes. She did as I asked her. She didn't know it yet, but I had brought her up there to consider asking her an important question. I got in the back seat beside her. She looked at me again but didn't say anything.

"I've brought you up here because I'm considering asking you to marry me. I've brought you up here so we could pray about it. I want you to pray. Go ahead and pray."

Though embarrassed and under pressure, she did offer a prayer, but it was the worst prayer I've ever heard in my life. I then offered what I thought was a sincere prayer—this proposal was something I had thought about for some time.

She was only too eager to get back in the front seat. As I myself sat down, I said to myself, *You really blew that. She will never speak to you again.*

We drove down the canyon in silence. I drove Shirley to her apartment, she opened the car door and was gone in a flash.

When I got back to my apartment, my brother asked me, "You home already?"

"Yep."

"Where'd you go?"

When I told my roommates what I'd done, they laughed until midnight. "Man, you are the craziest, dumbest guy we've ever heard of. You just don't do things like *that*!"

I never contacted Shirley again for several days. I believed it was now all over. My only thought was, *Lord, I blew that. Still, I'd like to marry her. I don't love her, but if she's got these qualities, I'd still like to marry her. I think she'd be a good wife, a good mother. She's also from the farm… .*

Shirley went home for the weekend, and the team was about to go back east to play. I still figured I'd blown everything, messed everything up.

The basketball team went back east and played in the National Invitation Tournament. At her home on the farm that weekend, Shirley happened to listen to the BYU basketball game on KSL Radio. Her father came in the house from milking and asked her, "Why are you listening to the ballgame? That's a bunch of nonsense—a ball game. You should be helping with the chores."

She replied, "I'm going to marry the guy who's playing."

That's actually what she said! And she hadn't seen me for two or three weeks. However bad that night had been, in those few weeks, she had thought about it all and decided she was going to marry me.

About ten days later, after the team came back from the NIT, I happened to bump into Shirley as we were walking out of the old North Building. She was walking alone, and I walked along with her. It was a friendly occasion. "Why don't we go for a ride?" I asked her.

"Let's go."

"I really shouldn't skip my class," I said. But I did.

We drove up to Kamas to visit my uncle, but he wasn't home. So I took her to a restaurant there and bought her a little something to eat. On the way down through Francis and Heber, I said to Shirley, "I want to apologize for being a jerk."

"Oh, that's all right."

"But I really am serious about wanting to marry you."

"Oh, I'm serious about it too."

Some people laugh about it all and think it was goofy, but three weeks later she was ready to marry me, and we became engaged.

I dated Shirley only three or four times before we got engaged, and that upset her father, who'd been paying her way through school. His attitude was that if she was going to get married, he would no longer support her in school. So she went back up to the farm in Benson, Utah, northwest of Logan, while I stayed at BYU.

That summer, I worked for the Forest Service in Wyoming, fighting forest fires and building trails—a good job. I was in the mountains, seeing bear, elk, and other animals all summer long.

When I returned to school that fall, Shirley's father still said he would not pay her way back to school, so she came down to Provo and got a job for a while. Then she returned to Benson, though she and her parents would come down to all our basketball games.

That Christmas we were engaged, the team was going back east on a ball trip, and I wanted to buy Shirley some kind of Christmas present. But I wasn't very good at doing those kinds of things. I did remember that when I came back from work that summer, Shirley and I went downtown to buy some little thing. We were in J.C. Penney's, which was having some kind of a clearance on coats. She looked at a coat and said, "Boy, that looks good. I'd like to have it."

"You've got it," I said to her, and I bought it for her. I'd never shopped for a present for anybody.

I remembered that Shirley liked to sew, so I asked a friend of hers, "Marie, what would Shirley like for a Christmas present?"

"She'd like a sewing machine."

I went over to the Singer sewing machine store and asked the clerk, "If I bought a sewing machine here, could you deliver it to Benson, Utah, sometime before Christmas?"

"Yes, we can arrange that. We'll deliver it the day before Christmas."

I gave them Shirley's address and bought the sewing machine. I don't remember how much of my meager wages I paid down, though I did get it paid for before we married.

Herschel married Shirley Falslev in Logan, Utah on March 18, 1955.

Before I left on the ball trip, I called Shirley up at her home. "How are you doing? Merry Christmas."

She started to cry.

"What's wrong?"

"They've just barely delivered my sewing machine. I'm so happy you thought of buying that for me."

We married on March 19, 1955, in the Logan Temple where her uncle was the second counselor in the temple presidency.

Our marriage day turned out to be a bad day for me. I hadn't been to the temple for a long time. We were to be married at nine o'clock in the morning and Shirley hadn't taken out her endowment, so we had to be there early. Then her uncle took us into his office and talked to us for about forty-five minutes because we were family. I was nervous. He told me not to worry. Everything would be all right.

Finally, Shirley was brought to us. "You're going to be the witness couple," her uncle announced—Shirley's first time at the temple, and they're asking her to be a witness!

I said, "I don't know what a witness couple does." Everything was memorized in those days; there was no film.

I was told, "Don't worry. The temple worker will tell you what to do."

There were more delays, and I couldn't understand why. Even by the time the session was over, I was still confused. With everybody lecturing us, we didn't get out of the temple till two in the afternoon.

Shirley's sisters had prepared a big dinner at the home, and there was quite a crowd. And then there was the reception.

My old, gray 1951 Chevrolet, which I called the "Gray Panther," had a lot of miles on it, and I knew somebody was going to paint it up—that was the tradition among all my friends and the people who'd come up from BYU for the reception.

Shirley and I stood in line for what seemed like an eternity. The reception was supposed to start at seven and end at nine, but we were still standing there at ten-thirty. People just kept hanging around.

Then someone announced: "We're going to take you over to Maddox's in Brigham City for a wedding breakfast."

My old car wouldn't start: the tires were flat, the engine was dead (I later learned that somebody had taken the distributor cap off), and it was all painted up. Everybody was laughing, and I didn't know what to do. "I've got to get this car started," I insisted. My father-in-law had an electric tire pump that I was going to borrow. But everybody said, "No, don't go." But we did.

By the time we were out of the "wedding breakfast" (actually a dinner) at Maddox's, it was nearly one o'clock in the morning.

On the way back to Logan, Westin Henry, who was teaching high school in Logan at the time, said to us, "Here, you take my brand-new car. Your car's all broke down, so take my car to the motel where you're going to stay. Come to my place in the morning and I'll help you get your car started."

We started our marriage off with a prayer, and now I'm praying with my wife. But the only things that came into my mind were the things I'd been saying when I prayed alone. Somehow during all those years of praying, I'd never thought about what I would pray for when I was married. I finally did say a prayer, and Shirley also offered a prayer. It was probably two or three years before I was able to pray about things I wanted to with Shirley.

The next morning, we drove over to Westin Henry's place, where bacon and eggs and pancakes and everything else had been fixed. All the missionaries came over too. Then we went to Shirley's house in Benson to get the presents and the car. There was my car at the front of the driveway, ready to go. We drove to our little basement apartment in Provo, which we had rented for $37.50 a month.

That was how our marriage started. We attended the Bonneville Ward in Provo. I still had another year of basketball at BYU. I worked at Geneva Steel that summer. The Forest Service had offered me a job as a "smoke watcher," and we could live all summer in a cabin in the mountains. But Shirley didn't want to do that.

Shirley was soon pregnant, and we didn't have insurance. We saved money for the baby. Coach Watts recommended Glen Allen as a doctor. When we went to see him, he said the fee would be $125, and we could just come in every three or four weeks, without even making an appointment. Shirley worked at the Barbizon clothing factory.

Shirley drove the car to work. My brother Herbert had an old Jeep without a gas tank, so I tied a five-gallon can of gas between the seats and ran a siphon hose into the gas line. That's what I drove back and forth to Geneva all that summer, where I worked in the blast furnace as a laborer.

Our first baby was born in December. The hospital also charged $125. (We eventually had nine children in all. They are all boys, except the last eight.)

Chapter Seven

Varsity Basketball at BYU

When I was a freshman, BYU had tried to convert me from a guard to a center, but I was third string. I started four or five games as a guard, but the rest of the time I sat on the bench. Toward the end of my career at BYU, I played most of the time.

My sophomore year, a player from the University of New Mexico, Tony Robles, had to be the best shooter I'd ever seen. He was averaging 45 points a game, and New Mexico was coming to play at BYU. We had no trouble with them here, so when we visited New Mexico, our coach figured it could be a tough game. "We're going to let Robles have his 45 points, but we're going to stop everyone else. We'll win the game because they'll only get those 45 points."

Harry Anderson, who was also the conference sprint champ, defined our defense, but Harry was about four inches shorter than Robles. Being so fast, he could cut Robles off and force him to shoot from farther out than normal. Still, Robles could shoot over Harry. The concern of the rest of our team was to shut everyone else down.

With Harry on him, Robles started missing the bucket and scored only 23 points. We beat New Mexico twice as badly there as we had on our home court.

That year, Wyoming had a tall team. The shortest of the four was 6′ 9″, and the two others were 6′ 11″. At 6′ 7′, I was BYU's tallest man. (Wyoming's little guard, Joe Capua, set a conference single-game scoring record the following year with 56 points.)

My senior year, we had never beaten Wyoming in their home court because of these big players, though we'd always beat them at BYU. So in preparation for the final game, we practiced hard and committed ourselves to hustle more. Our front line consisted of Ed Pinegar, at about 6′ 5″, and John Benson, about the same height. We also had as guards Harry Anderson and Terry Tebbs. Tebbs was a short guy, but he had the longest arms you'd ever see. When he went for the ball, his arms would keep extending. He would be guarding Joe Capua, who was then leading the conference in scoring, putting in 40 to 50 points a game.

I got the opening tip by using a couple of tricks I won't mention (because they're not what you'd call sportsmanlike today). The tip went to Tebbs, but when I came down, I slipped and fell. Tebbs passed the ball to me just above the top of the foul circle, but I was being double-teamed. To this day I don't know why I did what I did, but I threw a jump shot, and boom! It went right in, just like the ball had eyes in it. But I wasn't supposed to shoot those long shots.

The next time down the court, here were the three big guys, and they had me pretty well blocked off, though I did get a tip-in, which they didn't even contest. A minute later, there was a foul shot. I asked the 6′ 11″ guy, "How come you didn't take the rebound?"

"We're all ticked off at the coach.'

"What do you mean, 'ticked off at the coach'?"

"He wants Capua to break the scoring record against you guys tonight—he wants him to get 56 points against you, so we're not supposed to shoot. We're the front line, but the coach wants us to give him the ball all the time. But we're not going to do it."

I called time-out and went over to Coach Watts: "Coach, there's some dissension on that team. One of Wyoming's big men told me that the big guys aren't even hustling, not even trying, because they're ticked off at the coach, who wants Capua to break the scoring record against us."

BYU Basketball Team, 1953-54. Herschel is second from the right, back row.

"I'll watch them for a minute," the coach said.

What did we do? We took Harry Anderson off the other guard—who wasn't going to be shooting—and put him on Capua, and Harry was twice as fast. Capua would be dribbling around out about twenty-five to thirty feet, and when the big guys got the ball, they'd just throw it back to Capua.

In the meantime, no matter what I threw up, it went in. I didn't miss a shot the whole first half, and we had by then a 15- or 17-point lead. Capua only had about eight or ten points.

Our locker room was on the other side of the wall from theirs, and you could hear their lockers slamming and the Wyoming coach was screaming and cussing. Coach Watts commented, "I think we'll just sit here and listen to Wyoming."

The coach slammed the big man, who had been guarding me, up against a locker. "That Pedersen's got all those points, and you don't even have one point. *He's* the one who's going to break the record tonight. We're going out there and beat these guys," he screamed. We just sat there and listened to him through the wall.

Finally Coach Watts told us, "Everyone start playing ball. Bones, you're hot, so you just keep putting points up. We'll give you the ball and you do what you want to do."

We had a play that the coach called "the clear at the side." Everybody would clear out, I'd set up on the opposite side of the ball, one of the guards or Pinegar would set a screen, and then I'd come out and try to catch the ball in the key. There'd be nobody else around me except the guy guarding me.

After halftime, the morale of the Wyoming players was so low, it didn't matter what I'd do when I got the ball. I'd fake, but the guy guarding me would just stand there, so I'd go around him and make lay-ups. So the Wyoming coach took him out and put in some juniors, guys we'd never played before.

We ended up winning by about 25 points. It was probably the best game of my life. I'd married by then and had a child a few months old.

Maybe my best game was against Colorado State when I was a junior. Art Hughes, who had played with Coach Watts at BYU, had become the CSU coach after coaching at Snow College, in Ephraim, Utah. The coaches were thus good friends with each other. By then, Ed Pinegar had become a starter, and team morale was high, because one of our team who hadn't been living BYU standards was no longer on the team.

His first year, Hughes had a pretty rough season. He had some good players, but I could block his center's hook shots.

Colorado State's gym at that time was long and narrow. Colorado could put up a good defense, because there was no place for you to go on the court, and they played a tight zone. So Coach Watts, during pre-game practice, said to me, "Bones, you're not going to get the ball much tonight. Coach Hughes will be running a zone against us and will shut you out. You set kind of a screen at the high post and let Tebbs and the other guys shoot from the perimeter. You're not a good shooter from the corner, only from the front."

I said, "Okay."

We fell behind four or five points about half way through the first half, and I had only two points. Realizing I wasn't going to get any points that night, if we were going to win that ballgame, we'd have to get the offensive rebounds. I knew that Tebbs would shoot, but Anderson wouldn't, so I wouldn't have to worry about rebounds if Anderson had the ball. Pinegar and John Benson would shoot, and so would another guard, if he came in. So every time Tebbs got the ball, I would start moving toward the basket so I could tip the ball in if he missed.

When Colorado State came to play BYU, I'd run down the outside of the court as fast as I could on a fast break. Normally Tebbs would pass the ball to Anderson and he would make a lay-up. But the other team anticipated that, so on a three-on-two fast break, Anderson passed the ball to me. Because only shorter guards were down the court on the defense, if a lay-up was missed, I could get the rebound and put the ball back in the hoop.

One time as I came down the court at full speed, the ball came to me, and, unable to pull up, I just planted my left foot and kind of threw a shovel pass right up from the floor. It went right in, and the fans began to laugh. It was one of those nights when everything you shoot goes in.

I also learned a good lesson about sportsmanship that night.

With about eleven minutes to go in the second half, we had a big lead. Coach Watts called me out of the game and said, "Boy, you're having a big night." Then the fans started chanting: "We want Bones! We want Bones!" But the coach said to me, "You can't go in. Other guys have a right to play."

The fans were cheering because the program said that I needed only one point to tie the field house scoring record, and two to break it.

Coach Watts reminded me, "We don't break records against our friends." Coach Art Hughes of Colorado State had been his teammate in college.

I replied, "That's right." And I never did break the record or come even close again. The great thing about that was the coach's unwillingness to break records that might embarrass his friends. I learned a lesson in sportsmanship from him and always admired him for his policy.

The center for Colorado State had a very good hook shot, so I pressured him from the back, and that caused the fans to snicker a little. I thought maybe I should back off, but I didn't want the coach to pull me out of the game; I was just beginning to start games. Still, I wanted to block his hook shot, and I knew I was just a step quicker than he was.

I got the opening tip, but after about three minutes, the other team had a three-point lead. When you watch a team play, you see things—you know just about what that team is going to do, when and where the ball's going to go. So I knew the ball was coming to the center, and I was directly behind him. I thought I could anticipate a pass to him.

Sure enough, I saw the pass coming. As I started around him the ball came in kind of low. I reached my hand through his legs, grabbed the ball, and pushed it to the floor. Then I held my left hand in the air, waving to the referee, waiting for him to call a jump ball.

The coach was now screaming, and my head was bumping the center's legs. That's when the fans started laughing again—they'd never seen anything like that.

The coach called a time out. I told him, "Coach, I'm trying to play serious." He assured me, "That was a good play. Stay in the game." I played the whole game, and we won that game, despite my antics.

The fans stopped laughing so much, and we won the game, though we lost to that team on their court, and also lost to Wyoming there, so we tied with the University of Utah for second in the conference that year. Wyoming was third.

We went out to eat after winning the game, and Coach Hughes was being interviewed on the news. When asked what had happened, he said, "Our scouting report was that all Pedersen could do was shoot a hook and a jump shot. Nobody told us he was an offensive rebounder. So we primed everything not to let him shoot. He didn't shoot much, but he tipped in twelve rebounds. He's the best rebounder I've seen in the conference. We won't make that mistake again."

Also in my junior year, I played three games (two of them against UCLA) when professional scouts were in attendance. All the newspapers were saying how UCLA was going to slaughter us, because they'd been fourth or fifth in the NCAA tournament the year before, and one of their All-Americans, who later played professional, was on the team.

In the locker room before the game, I showed a little levity—a little of the fun side of me. Sensing this, Coach Watts said, "Okay, guys, it's time to get serious"—but I knew he was talking to me. As I walked past him, I said, "Coach, we're gonna win this game. In fact, we're going to beat UCLA twice this year."

"That's the attitude," he said. "We're playing against a good team."

But I knew I shouldn't have said what I said. I hadn't been concentrating on the game, and I knew it. Tebbs and Anderson looked at me like I was goofy anyway.

BYU'S OWN 'GLOBETROTTERS'

When we were seniors, we were invited to play in some kind of tournament in Livingston, Montana, to raise money for the city. Only seniors of college teams were invited, and we didn't take a coach with us. The city paid our expenses, and if you won, players got a hundred dollars apiece. Six of us who had come along as freshmen won the tournament, and I was chosen Most Valuable Player.

After the tournament, there was a meeting with all the teams. Players were asked what we could do to improve the tournament. The Montana State Coach said, "We don't want you to invite BYU back again unless they'll train at Bar 19 with the rest of us."

Of course we didn't drink or smoke. We just played basketball and went back to the hotel and did our studies—school was still on. The other teams were down drinking, carousing, and spending money in the town.

Everybody laughed, and the town said they would invite us back again. There wouldn't be a rule to go down to Bar 19. It was all quite a joke.

I got so I could shoot. In fact, I was always first or second in scoring, and first or second in rebounding. I actually led the conference in shooting percentage. At one time, I held seventeen records at BYU, and some of them lasted for years. Of course they've all been broken since.

I played two and a half years as a starter, because I played only half of the season my sophomore year. I could out-jump other guys, and I had a pretty quick first or second step. I would lean one way and kind of look at the other guy's feet. Then as I leaned to the left, I would stretch my right foot back around him and kind of cross his leg a little. When I came back and planted my foot, my first step would be on the right side of his right foot. If he went to slide (as you're taught to do), he couldn't step out with his right foot because my right foot was blocking him. He'd either stumble or have to try to go around me, and that would delay him just long enough that I could get what was called a *spin move*. I'd wheel around and go for a lay-up.

These were kind of little "dirty tricks" we all pulled.

My junior year, we also had on the team Dean Larson, an All-American, as well as Tom Karen and Sherm Crump. We had a simple play, called the "rub-off." I'd set up the offense on the baseline underneath the basket, opposite the ball. Then I'd automatically pass the ball to whichever guard came down the opposite side. My responsibility was to rub off the opposing player, who would either have his back to me or was sideways to me, waving his head back and forth as he watched the ball go back and forth across the top of the key.

As soon as he went one way, I'd go the other, pop past him, and get the ball about ten or twelve feet out while he was still a few feet behind me. I made my first seven shots, then missed two. I ended up with about 20 points that night and some 22 rebounds. We won the game by about 12 points. I scored more points the second night, and we beat UCLA a second time.

Jim Murray, of the *Los Angeles Times*, wrote an article that was reprinted in the *Provo Daily Herald*. Coach Watts brought the article to me, which said, "Willie Knowles, the UCLA All-American, touted to be one of the top draft picks, was shown up by a person nobody had ever heard of—Herschel 'Soupbones' Pedersen. He out-rebounded Knowles, out-defensed him, and in general out-played him."

After the Bradley game my sophomore year, as we were sitting in the hotel lobby waiting to be taken to the airport, the game was being announced on a sporting show. The coach from Bradley introduced a pro scout who'd been at the game. He asked the scout, "Did you see anybody on either of these teams who looked like a pro?"

"Yeah," the scout said, "that big Pedersen kid that plays for BYU. We're interested in him."

That was the first time we heard about my being drafted. I ended up being drafted by the St. Louis Hawks.

My senior year, we really blew a game against Utah. We'd beaten them at Utah, and we had about a twelve-point lead in Provo with only three minutes to go. Both I and Tebbs had four fouls, and we were the leading scorers. Then the coach took us out. Utah started a press, and boom, boom, boom, they started putting the ball in the basket.

We still had a six-point lead when Tebbs and I went back it, but that didn't help. We ended up losing by two points to Utah, which meant we tied with them for the conference championship.

The worst game I ever played was against Utah State, whose coach was my former high school coach. I'd had good games against Utah State until I married. All my wife's brothers and sisters and other relatives from Cache Valley would come to the games and root for Utah State. And they razzed me continuously, especially Harold and Larry. They'd actually been on my case all summer long, especially when I went up there and hauled hay with them.

I had resolved to have a good night. I even prayed and fasted about it. I was so uptight I went after the ball like a wild man. I got the opening tip and came down the floor. Terry Tebbs was guarding Pat Dunn, a great ball player. He came by Tebbs, so I went to pick him up—but I fouled him. I had fouled him three times the first three minutes of the game. I spent most of the game on the bench in foul trouble.

With about five minutes left in the game, I was sitting on the bench with four fouls and four points. I went back in with three minutes left and made one more point. That was my worst game because I played only a few minutes.

My second worst game happened my senior year. Coach Watts had got tickets for Shirley's brothers and sisters, all of them were now sitting with the BYU ticket holders. Every time I went down the court, they hollered at me. I played a lousy game, ending up with only about 14 points, and we lost. I just couldn't do anything when we played Utah State in Logan.

Coach Watts didn't like me to dribble, though we practiced dribbling all the time. This "policy" led to a very funny experience when we played Montana. We always beat Montana, but in this one game, we had about a seven-point lead with three minutes to go. Coach Watts called a timeout and asked us to go into what we called a control offense, where we'd try to make the other team think we were stalling. (There was no shot clock in those days.) Then we'd break the game open with a few cheap lay-ups.

As soon as we got the ball, we went into that offense. Then the coach said to me, "Bones, when you get the rebound, don't dribble. I don't care where you are, stop, get the ball to the guards, and we'll go down and run that offense."

I said, "Okay."

Well, Eddie Anderson, Montana's ace shooter (he could pour the ball in from 25 to 30 feet), parked himself and launched one of his long scissor-balls from way out. It missed, the rebound came to me at about the foul line, and there was only one guy between me and our basket. Tebbs was coming down the other side of the court, but one dribble and I was nearly to the half-court line. Two dribbles and I was headed into the foul line. As we past the bench, Coach Watts jumped up and hollered, "Bones, I said pass the ball!"

As I went to throw it to Tebbs, it slipped out of my hands and went into about the tenth row of the bleachers.

The coach called a timeout. He was frustrated! I should have given the ball to Tebbs or Anderson as soon as I took the rebound, then gone down to set up the play.

The standing joke around BYU for a long time was, "You'd better take the side baskets down when the game comes to a close, or Bones will be trying to hit one of those instead of the basket that counts."

In another game with Montana, we found ourselves behind ten points at halftime. Coach Watts said, "We're going to post up and run the 'clear the side' play. Bones, we're going to give you the ball. We'll clear everybody out, and I think you can beat your guy one on one."

The guys pass me the ball at half court, while three of them stay on the perimeter. The closest defenseman to me is about ten feet away. My thought is, *The coach has put his trust in me. He's going to count on me.* I take one step and put in a hook shot. And then two more times down the court and two more hook shots.

The coach calls a timeout and tells us, "They're probably going to go into a zone or put a man in front of Bones to stop the pass. Just block him off and we'll give Bones the ball on the other side."

I think, *That's pretty good. He's still going to give me the ball.*

Sure enough, the bounce pass comes in from Burgess, I take one step on my right foot and lay the ball up with my left hand. I end up with 25 points in the second half.

After Dean Larsen, Tom Karen, and Sherm Crump had graduated, we had a game with Utah. Monday night the coach announces, "We're going to put in a new play, one we've never run before. Bones, you're the best shooter in the conference. That's because they were all short shots. So we're going to give you the ball and let you shoot against Utah."

All week long, I'm running the screen and shooting 25 to 30 shots every practice. Later in the game, we run the play. I get the ball, but talk about being uptight—I miss... and miss...and miss. I haven't hit a shot tonight, and I can't get the rebound because two guys are there screening me out, and another four are crowding the basket.

The coach says, "You just keep shooting."

But I miss again, and now it's halftime and we're twelve points behind.

The coach reassures me again: "I think you've got to get the butterflies out of you, so keep shooting."

By now I'm feeling bad.

We come back in the second half, run the play, and the ball goes in. I begin hitting every shot, and we beat Utah. The point is that even though I was missing shots, the coach had the confidence to say to me, "Sooner or later, the shot will start falling for you." Coach Watts was something of a father figure. Even when you were having a bad day, he'd say something like "keep shooting."

Our first trip after Christmas was in Manhattan, New York, and I played a total of six seconds. Nick Matelgan committed a foul, was pulled out, and so I lined up for a missed foul shot, got the rebound, the whistle blew, and I was out of the game. Six seconds had ticked off the game clock.

That didn't bother me. My main goal now was to get through school and on with my life. I had no complaints: I was eating the same meals as the rest of the team, going to the same games, getting the same treatment. I'd been on the army team, so I was now kind of a happy camper. I loved the game, I practiced hard, and I loved practice as much as I did the ball games.

Now the conference season had started, and I'd moved up to the second team. We were getting ready to play the University of Denver. That's when I almost got kicked off the team.

The game was way out of hand—we were far ahead of Denver. Their center, Dick Brott, a sophomore (the same as I was) was the leading rebounder in the conference at the time. With only four or five minutes left in the game, and us with a 20 to 25 point lead, I was put in to play. Knowing that no matter what I did we couldn't lose, I decided to have some fun. So I did some goofy things, and pretty soon the fans were laughing. I wasn't trying to make them laugh, but now, no matter what I did, they laughed.

I'd bump Brott, push him around. We got to bumping each other, and soon the referee stopped us. I explained, "Hey, I'm just having a little fun. This game's over, and if I foul out, it's no big deal to me."

But Brott was getting a bit upset, and pretty soon the referee called a double foul. At that time, after the foul shot at each end, you had a jump ball. Brott was standing at the foul line. I walked up to the referee, who still had the ball, and asked, "In a double foul, does it matter who shoots the foul shot first?"

He said no.

So I took the ball and said, "Then I'll shoot mine first." I took the ball to the other end, and that made the fans laugh.

When the game was over, Coaches Millet and Watts, and trainer Eddie Kimball, took me in a room by myself. Millet asked me, "What were you doing out there?"

"Coach, I was just having fun."

Coach Watts was more perturbed: "I have never seen anything like that on the court in my life. We will not tolerate it. This isn't a comedy. We're playing ball."

"But I was just having some fun."

They talked to me for about twenty or thirty minutes, and that left me pretty sober. I was given to understand that if I expected to play ball, I would never do anything like that again. I would play ball the way I was taught, the way we did it in practice. They told me I would not get in the game the next night against New Mexico.

Sure enough, I would not get to play that night because of the antics I had pulled the night before. Warm ups were complete and we had returned from the dressing room for a final three minutes of shooting before the game was to begin. I went to the end of the bench, sat down and put my feet up on the apron of the playing floor. I leaned back and relaxed to watch the ball game. The game was less than three minutes into the first quarter when the crowd started chanting, "We want Bones! We want Bones!" The chants continued for about four minutes and I became embarrassed and could do nothing but sit there.

I slid down in my chair trying to avoid any attraction. The players sitting by me said, "Boy, you're going to get it in practice next week." My fear was that it might be serious enough to get kicked off the team. I glanced up the road and Coach Watts scowled at me, and I knew his blood was beginning to boil.

It's about three minutes to go in the half, and the ballgame is getting more and more out of hand. The fans are hollering. They'd seen what I'd done in the Denver game the night before. I'm sitting on the end of the bench, cowering, along with Willard Hirshi and Ed Pinegar, all of us sophomores, not even daring to look up at the coach. All of us are usually put in the game last, except Blaine Anderson, the starting center. Those guys are looking at me, so I say, "When this game is over, I'll be kicked off the team. Listen to the fans. They've really got me in trouble." I was terrified.

Herschel celebrating the victory after the BYU-Utah game in 1955.

Then suddenly Coach Watts says, "Bones, get in there!"—in a way that I know he is serious. "I'm putting you in there not because I want to, I want you to shut these fans up. If you do one thing that makes them laugh, you'll be back on the bench, and you'll never play again."

I says, "Yes, Sir."

The fans start cheering and clapping, and I haven't even got to the scorer's bench, way down off the apron of the playing floor. There's a little area where you stand before you walk out on the floor. After I report, the scorer says, "Get out of my way. I can't see."

So I move over a bit, but then Coach Watts, also nearby, says, "Get out of my way. You're in front of me, and I can't see."

Well, my usual seat is clear down at the end of the bench, so I can't go clear back down there. So what do I do? I just lay down on the floor and put my hand on my head—not trying to be funny or anything.

The fans start hollering, and Coach Watts looks at me—and he is really ticked off.

The whistle finally blows and I go into the ball game, while the fans now start clapping.

It's now half time, and I get ripped on for laying down on the court. I say to the coach, "Coach, there was no place else to sit."

From that time on, all the players moved down one seat and left an empty chair by the coach. That's when BYU started that custom. It hadn't been done that way before.

I ended up playing quite a bit the second half and scored about 12 points. But it didn't matter what I did, the fans laughed. Toward the end of the game, when all the sophomores were being put in—Ed Pinegar, Lynn Rowe, Willard Hirschi, Lloyd Rasmussen, Harry Anderson and Tom Stancke (there were about seven sophomores on the ball club)—we were doing pretty good.

Whenever we came down the court with the ball, the coach would signal the guards the play we were supposed to run. This time, we were going to run a certain high-post play. I was supposed to break up to the high post, and the forward would come off the back door. Willard Hirschi was the conference hurdle champ, Harry Anderson, the other guard, the conference sprint champ, but he didn't shoot. Hirschi agreed that as soon as I went to the high post, he'd be cutting to the basket.

Hirschi cut all right, but about a second before he was supposed to. The ball was still being passed to me. When it hit me, I threw it back over my head, without even looking. He'd said he'd be there get it, and he was. He put it in the basket.

The fans, thinking I was showboating, started to laugh again. And boy, I was in bad trouble.

Coach Watts took me out. I said to him, "Coach, I tried to be serious. I didn't try to make those people laugh."

"Forget about it," he assured me. "You'll be all right."

From then on, I became a starter on the team.

Monday morning when the newspapers came out, John Mooney of the *Salt Lake Tribune* wrote, "We don't need the Globetrotters in Utah, we've got Bones Pedersen at BYU. He's a better show than the Globetrotters."

As a starter, I didn't do many more goofy things. I had to settle down, and that's what I did till the end of my BYU career. Still, I had fun playing ball—I believe I had more fun than anybody who ever played the game, because I loved the game. To me, it was like watching a funny movie or something.

KENTUCKY GAME

When I played for BYU, I was listed at being six feet, nine inches tall. I asked the coach, "Where do they get these figures from?"

Cal Clark was a great basketball player for the University of Kentucky. As we were going over the scouting report for the game, Coach Watts said to me, "This Clark guy is a great player on the outside. He can shoot great. He's fast. But look, he's twenty-five years old, just an old man. You don't have to worry about him."

I raised my hand and said, "Coach, I'm twenty-five years old too, and I once played against him when I was in the army and he was in the air force. I'll tell you, he's a great basketball player. He scored about 25 points against us."

An interesting thing happened in that ball game. The referees, all from the Big Ten conference, called us together at the middle of the court and said, "We're going to call this game very strictly. Any sign of unsportsmanlike conduct will be a technical foul. Any call you question will be a technical. Now go out and play the game."

Kentucky's guard came down the court. Terry Tebbs slapped at the ball and missed. Even though he didn't foul the guy, the referees called a foul. Terry put his hands on his hips, and I guess the referee interpreted that as disgust or disagreement. He got a technical called on him. In those days, a technical foul was not counted against you as a personal foul, like it does now.

The coach said to us, "Just keep your mouths shut. Just raise your hand when a foul is called on you."

Now both teams are keeping their mouths shut. We were on the Kentucky end of the floor, and the ball was passed to their center. I kind of reached around to steal it, without touching him. But the whistle blew. I raised my hand, turned my back, and started to walk down to line up at the foul circle.

The referee walked past me and said, "You thought I missed that call, didn't you? You know that I made a bad call, don't you?"

"I didn't say anything, Sir," I explained, then just looked the other way.

My thought was, *That rude guy.*

Now we were down at the other end of the court. I put up a hook shot, and the whistle blew. The referees called a foul on the guy guarding me, even though he hadn't fouled me.

The referee walked up to me and said, "That evens it up, Mister."

That kind of thing happened in ball games.

REFEREE STORY

In a game with the University of Utah, Fred Sanford, one of the Skyline Conference officials, was refereeing. He'd been a great athlete at the U. We had a three-point lead, with about a minute and a half to go. The ball went out of bounds, and I was to pass it in.

There was old Fred, the sweat running down his face. I said to him, "Fred, why don't you relax? It's just a lousy ball game. Ten years from now, nobody will remember the score, or that I played, or that you even blew a whistle in this game. Just have fun like I'm doing."

About fifteen years later, when I was playing in a Church volleyball game in Salt Lake City, Fred, now retired from refereeing college basketball, was now refereeing volleyball. He came up to me and said, "I want to thank you."

"For what, Fred?" I asked.

"You were playing at Utah one time, and you said something to me that helped me out more than anything else in life. I was always worried about making a wrong call. I was always worried about being blackballed as a referee. You told me to relax and have fun, not to worry about such things—that nobody would remember that I had even refereed a game."

"That's right," I said. "Nobody remembers such things, though I do remember that you were the referee in that game. But that ballgame doesn't count anymore."

That was kind of my attitude. I mean, I liked to win, but when we lost, I didn't go around sad-faced. It was just a ball game. I played. I had fun."

All the time I played ball at BYU, my father came to my games or listened to them on the radio. If we lost, he'd have a bad day the next day, though losses never bothered me. Coach Watts would give the players so many tickets. On one special occasion my senior year, he gave me ten tickets, so cousins, uncles and aunts came down to the game.

PROFESSIONAL OFFER

The St. Louis Hawks, owned by Anheiser Busch, offered me a three-year professional contract, with a no-cut clause. That meant I'd become their employee and do promotional work. Part of the contract was that in the off season, I would do promotional work for the beer company.

I told my wife, "I can't do that."

I wrote the Hawks a letter in which I said I didn't think I'd play for them. Maybe I could be traded to someone else? The answer came back: "You play for us or you don't play for anybody."

In those days, there wasn't the trading of players like there is now. Nor were the wages then like they are now. Basketball professionals at that time were paid only between $25,000 and $30,000 a year, five times the contract I was offered by Geneva Steel, an offer I accepted. There were several things wrong with the basketball contract. They are professionals, they are in a business, their objective is to make money, and many of the games were on Sundays. Add to that the travel, living in hotels, being with teammates who drank, smoked and chased women and the commercials I would have to do in the off season. If you didn't lower your standards and participate, you became an outsider.

I was now twenty-six years old, and Geneva Steel had offered me a job in management. When I saw the retirement package at Geneva, I said to my wife, "Why don't we spent thirty or thirty-five years there, and then we'll just go on missions the rest of our lives?"

As my wife and I now think of that decision, we remember all the good experiences we had at Geneva Steel. Recently, in fact, as I was coming out of sacrament meeting, there was one of the pipe fitters from the plant. He'd drunk coffee, smoked, and drunk a little alcohol. Now he'd been through the temple with is daughter and held a position in the Church.

These are the kind of people whose lives my wife and I have affected, and that means a lot more than playing basketball. I'd never have been a good pro basketball player anyway. I'd have been a worrier.

My wife and kids will tell you that I'm the world's champion worrier, and having to play with a bunch of guys who were immoral, who drank and caroused, would have upset me to the point that I wouldn't have been able to play well. When I see people doing something wrong, I try to find a way to correct it. I'd have preached to those sinners and would probably have caused dissension on the team—that's the way I've been all my life. I'd have offended people, and that's what would have happened in professional basketball. I'd have ended up a nervous wreck.

Above all, my purpose in life was not to play basketball; my purpose was to do something worthwhile. So my basketball career ended, though I played some church basketball and played in the Orem Recreation League with some other workers at Geneva.

By my last year at BYU, 1956, I'd played on three of BYU's teams. I never did seem to get tired. I could always go—I think that came from having worked on the farm. I had big hands, and I could especially jump—something I was blessed with.

One year while I played church ball, we won the all-Church tournament. Our final game was against the Mesa Eighth Ward. The score was tied at the end of the game, and the winner was the first to score next in sudden death. I threw in a hook shot. All the crowd packed me off the court—you'd have thought we'd won the national tournament.

When I was in the army during the Korean War, I also played volleyball, so I also had a great volleyball career, because of my big hands and my jumping ability, even though I'd never played volleyball except in my backyard. I finally learned to make a run, take a one-step jump, and spike the ball. When I was overseas, I was on the army team that won the All-Services Tournament in the Far East. I also won the post Ping-Pong tournament.

When I returned to BYU, I tried to get volleyball going there, but BYU only had intramural at that time. I later played volleyball in the Salt Lake County Recreation League and was voted Most Valuable Player. We went to the all-Church volleyball competition about ten years in a row, but the highest we ever got was fifth.

I was the only returned missionary on the team, and once in a while the coach would call me in to his office and say, "I'd like to talk to you about a certain ballplayer. You've got a little more maturity than the others, so it doesn't matter to you so much if you don't play. Such things don't bother you, but a lot of things bother these other kids."

I never did let it bother me to sit on the bench. I considered myself lucky to have even *made* the high school basketball team.

But other players, one in particular, a former All-State player, played only a few minutes a game. He had come to the coach in tears, saying he was going to quit school. "He'll be a starter when he's a senior," the coach explained to me. "But now he's only a sophomore. Will you talk to him or something?"

Other capable recruits had scrapbooks full of clippings, fans had been cheering them, but now they were sitting on the bench, and they couldn't handle it.

If I was in a hotel room alone, Rod Kimball, the trainer, might come to me and say, "I'd like to talk to you about such and such a problem this kid has with his family. Next trip, we're going to put you in the same hotel room with him for three or four days.

I'd go talk with these players who had problems, like a missionary would talk to a missionary who wanted to go home because he was homesick.

At BYU, I had the same scholarship, the same meals, as the other players. My sophomore year, I was voted the "most improved player" in the conference, and I made All-Conference second team. I was All-Conference my junior and senior years, and usually first or second in scoring and rebounding. My senior year, I made third-team All-American. That's when letters started coming in from professional teams, inviting me to a rookie camp.

Chapter Eight

Family

In December of my last year of school at BYU, our son was born. We didn't know what to name him. Shirley's parents came down and stayed with us a couple of days, though we only had a bed and a couch for all of us to sleep on. We let them sleep in the bed.

The next morning, Shirley's mother was sitting at the table, looking kind of sad. She said, "You know, I've always wanted to name one of my sons Wayne, but my husband wouldn't allow it."

That's how our son Wayne got his name, and it didn't bother us that she had picked it.

Wayne was born with a red spot between his eyes, a birthmark or mark left by the forceps. Shirley thought he looked like a little mouse when he was born—kind of pale and pink-skinned.

Thirteen months later, Shauna was born. I'd picked that name when I was in Japan in the military, playing basketball. My commanding officer in Special Services, Major Julian Phillips, a Baptist from Houston, Texas, invited me and Jim Walsh, the assistant to the Catholic chaplain, to Thanksgiving dinner. Walsh and I were good friends, and also starters on the base basketball team. The major had a beautiful wife and a beautiful daughter.

The major picked us up, we had dinner, and then he drove us back to our quarters. He said to me, "Bones, I want you to take my daughter out."

I replied, "I can't do that, Major."

"Why not?"

"I'm not going to date anybody that I can't marry in a Mormon temple, and your daughter's not a member of my church."

"That's got nothing to do with it. You're the only man I've met in the army who I'd let date my daughter, because I know she'd be safe with you. I want you to take her out."

In 1985, Herschel Pedersen was inducted into BYU's Sports Hall of Fame. Here he is pictured with his wife, their children and spouses.

A Captain Reese on the base also started inviting me over to dinner, and I found out that his wife was a member of the Church, though from being in the military, she wasn't active. I sometimes tended their children for them, and they had an eight-year-old girl named Shauna. That's why I ended up naming my daughter Shauna.

By then, we had moved out of the basement apartment and rented a little duplex behind Bill and Iva's Café in Orem. We were saving our money to buy a house.

Sheryl was the next child, even though the doctors and nurses had guaranteed the baby was going to be a boy. My brother Keith was with me at the hospital, and we were kind of uninhibited at times. We got two wheelchairs and started racing up and down the halls, while I sang the western song "It's a boy, it's a boy. I'm a father."

The nurses thought we were crazy, but then they came out and said, "It's a girl." I couldn't believe it, nor could the nurse—she said this was the first time she'd ever been wrong. The doctor had said he was hearing a slow heartbeat, and that's the sign of a boy. (All my children have a slow heartbeat. The last time I was tested, my heart rate was forty-eight beats a minute while I'm resting.)

We bought our present home in American Fork just before Sheryl was born.

We eventually ended up with eight girls and Wayne. Our girls' names all start with *Sh-*, after Shirley: Shauna, Sheryl, Sheila, Shelley, Sharlene, Sharon, Sharee, and Shirlynn.

Shirlynn's name was figured out by the kids in fast and testimony meeting when the baby was to be blessed. I handed one of the kids a card and said, "Figure out a name." Shirlynn is, in a way, a form of Shirley, but my wife didn't want the girl to be named Shirley.

Chapter Nine

Beginning Work at Geneva

The summer after we married, I was offered a job as a "smoke watcher" with the Forest Service, but as I've said earlier, Shirley didn't want to do that. Shirley was pregnant, and we didn't have insurance. We had to save our money for the baby.

The baby was born in December, and I finished school in the spring.

The day after I graduated in management from Brigham Young University, Geneva Steel offered me a job. (I'd actually been offered a job there earlier). The first day I worked in the office for four hours, and then I was taken down and introduced to the general foreman of the pig machine. He told me I would start out as the foreman there. I didn't even know what a "pig machine" was or where it was located. I received no training.

When I reported, I found I had a crew of ten men, but of course I didn't know what they did. I was a lost soul, if there ever was one.

My first night on the job, there was a problem with an iron ladle that came in from the Ironton plant, south of Provo, and I made a mistake that cost the company more than a hundred thousand dollars. I spent the rest of the night writing up what I'd done, and in the morning, I took the report up to the superintendent. My foreman was of course devastated, and I figured I'd be fired.

The superintendent read the report, looked at me, and said, "Well, we've all made worse mistakes than that one. Forget it. Just don't make another one."

Neither of these men was a Latter-day Saint, and that episode taught me a great lesson about forgiveness—to think that a mistake of that consequence could be overlooked.

The steel plant transferred me to different positions, and eventually I was trained to supervise the blast furnaces. As a result, I got to know everyone who worked in that department. Because I had played basketball at BYU, I had an "in" with the men, or at least some credibility. A lot of the men had been to basketball games, so I was treated a little better as a foreman than other foremen were. The men all wanted to talk basketball.

But because I was also a very religious individual, I found myself at odds with most of the people in management, who were either inactive, or even apostate Church members, or not members at all. I won't say I was persecuted or discriminated against; it's just that I didn't get some of the breaks that others sometimes got.

I may have brought all this on myself. I felt that men on the job who made mistakes should not be suspended and lose a day or more at work, or be severely reprimanded. If you suspended a man, you not only punished him, but also his wife and children, because you were maybe depriving them of food, clothes, medicine, education and other needs. I thought you could punish a man in such a way that you could get him to work according to the rules. You didn't need to punish his family.

That attitude was what first caused me difficulties with the management. Then I also began to do things to get some of the men active in the Church.

Everywhere I went in the plant, I found people who were inactive in the Church. Being bold, and maybe a little overly aggressive, I guess I took it upon myself (though I'd like to think the Lord inspired me) to talk to them. I've always found it easy to talk to people, and the workers who were active in the Church often sought me out, and we'd have gospel conversations. The inactives were also very friendly, but as soon as we started talking about the Church, a lot of them would find something else to do.

Still, I was terrified when I had to correct people. I didn't like to do that, even when I was in a position of leadership from my first day of work there. I just taught the gospel because that's the kind of person I was. I'd learned that on my mission. We'd knock on doors and I'd say, "We're going to get in." That's the attitude I took at my work at the plant.

I soon learned that if a bunch of men are sitting around talking at lunch hour, the best thing to do was to participate briefly in the conversation—get the men to talking about something and then just shut up and listen. The men would sometimes talk openly about their own problems, or their families' problem. Sometimes they would talk about the Church, and sometimes I even found myself saying something negative about the Church, just to get the inactives and anti-Church men to open up. My philosophy was, "You can't help anybody be a good person till you get all the poison out of them".

So if one of the guys started cussing a bishop, I'd say, "Well, I knew a bishop who did such and such one time"—some dinky little thing that didn't amount to much. Pretty soon I'd have a whole bunch of information to talk to these men about, and that became invaluable when I started to help them become active in the Church.

Some of the things I said even ingratiated me with the workers, I guess. An experience that happened in 1959, after I'd been there about three years, especially helped me. I wasn't having too much success activating the men, but then a long strike—150 days or so—put everybody off work, with no pay. When the strike ended, the pheasant hunting season was on, and I was in Logan, hunting. It was a Saturday morning, and the plant was calling us back to work. We were to report by seniority. One man was to be to work at eight o'clock on Sunday morning, but he was an alcoholic, he gambled, and he was immoral. His wife worked hard and had paid for the children's education, had sent the kids on missions, and had stayed with her husband.

I was assigned to go by his home at two in the morning and make sure his wife knew her husband was supposed to be at work at eight o'clock. If he couldn't make it, then I was to get someone to take his job.

I drove by his home and pounded on the door. His wife, in her nightgown, opened the door, but her husband was lying on the floor in the front room, drunk. Now I could be kind of a critical person—I had a hard time seeing why people couldn't live the Word of

Wisdom. But I looked at the wife and said, "You know, I've worked with your husband for three years. He does nothing but drink, gamble and step out on you, yet you've stayed with him all these years. You've paid all the bills. What makes you stay with him?"

She looked at me and started to cry. Then she choked out, "I love him, and you don't!"

That cut me to the very heart.

She said she'd have him to work the next morning, and he was there when I arrived. I said to him, "You've got to be the most ungrateful man I ever knew. To have a woman who loves you the way your wife loves you, and then to put her through all the trouble you have. You drink up every penny you make, or you gamble it away. She's paid the bills. She's sent your kids to school. And your kids are turning out pretty good. You need to do something for your wife, who's bestowed all her love on you and stuck with you. You ought to be ashamed of yourself!"

He didn't say anything, but about two or three weeks later, he came to me and asked, "How can I be good to my wife?"

"Number one," I said to him, "you could quit drinking. Number two, you could quit gambling. Be kind to her. Be the kind of man she'd like you to be. And you could start taking your money home to her so you could afford to take her on a nice trip. When you get home from that trip, your life will all straighten out. She wants to be married in the temple."

"Are you sure about that?" he asked me.

"Yeah. Any woman who loves you the way she does would not consider supporting your kids by sending them on missions unless she wanted to be married in the temple."

He began to think about that. It took him three or four months to put his life in order and become a better worker. The last time I saw him, he had retired and was an ordinance worker in the Provo Temple.

To be able to say something like that to another person means you have to develop some kindness and mercy, and that comes through prayer and reading the scriptures. At that time, I was reading all the standard works four times a year and memorizing scriptures—but memorizing is no good unless you use them on somebody. So I had been asking the Lord, "What can I say to his guy?" I found the answer in some verses in the D&C 100:5-8: "Speak the thoughts that I shall put into your hearts... For it shall be given you in the very hour, the very moment, what ye shall say. But a commandment I give unto you, that inasmuch as ye do this the Holy Ghost shall be shed forth in bearing record unto all things whatsoever ye shall say."

I figured that if I could appreciate this man and his wife for their potential, and feel the kind of love this woman had for her husband, maybe this man—and other men who weren't going to church—would start going to church.

About six months after this layoff, there was another layoff—Geneva had a lot of layoffs in the fall because the plant could hire people who had worked the summer vacations for the regular workers, and in that way these people could gain a little seniority. One young man at the plant got caught in a cutback, even though he was supposedly permanent. At age seventeen, he'd gotten a fifteen-year-old girl pregnant, and her parents hated him and his parents hated her. He was now about twenty and had a couple of kids. You could also say he was a little "slow," because he didn't read well, for lack of education.

He'd been off work three or four months, and when he came back, I was assigned to put some men to work on some spills out in the ore yard. When I went out about an hour later, he had hardly done anything. I kind of got after him, so he started shoveling again. But when I went out an hour later, he still had done hardly anything. It was now about eleven o'clock in the morning. I said to myself, *Lord, this guy was not a poor worker before. There's something wrong.*

I took him aside from the other guys. "What's the matter? You're just not working. Are you sick?"

"No, I am not sick. I just haven't had anything to eat in two days. I've been laid off work, and we don't have any money. My parents have refused to help us. My wife's parents have refused to help us. We've gone to the State but can't get help there. All I've got in the home is one loaf of bread and a gallon of milk, and we're letting the children eat that."

I thought to myself, *It is my obligation to help them.*

I took him to my office, where we were alone. I sat him down at my desk and said, "Here's my lunch. You eat every bit of it. Then you'll be ready to go out and do some work this afternoon."

He looked at me: "I shouldn't do that."

"No, you go ahead. I've got plenty of lunch when I get home."

After he ate my lunch, I called my wife to tell her what I'd done. I didn't think I should give away any money without her knowing it, so I said to her, "Now Dear, I know we're not the richest people in the world. We've got a lot of kids, but I've got a few dollars in my pocket. I'm going to give this boy all that money and tell him he's to go home and buy some food for his wife and kids, and then bring a lunch the next day."

I gave him $43.00—food was a lot cheaper in those days than it is now.

"I'm going to give you this money on one condition," I told him.

"What's that?"

"You go to church on Sunday."

"That's an amazing thing to ask me, but I'll do it."

The next day, I said to him, "You know, it's sad that you found yourself in that situation. Are your parents members of the Church."

"Oh, yeah. They go to church all the time.'

"And they won't help you?"

"No, they're mad at me because I got this girl pregnant and we got married, and we've got these kids, and they don't like my wife. And my wife's folks, they go to church too, but they don't like us and won't help us for the same reason."

"Well, that's too bad, but you've got to be a greater person than your parents or her parents are. If you had been going to church, the bishop would have helped you. I've helped you a little bit, and I'll help you the next time—until payday in two or three weeks."

When I saw him the next week after he'd gone to church, I asked him, "Well, how did you like church?"

"I didn't like it at all. And the kids are too small to sit through meetings."

"I'll tell you what. There's no way you're going to be happy in your situation. You've got to go to church, and you need to be married in the temple."

He went out and told the other workers what I'd said and done, and it was a favorable experiment—an advertisement, you might say.

Pretty soon his elders quorum president in Lindon was working with him. The kid started to say such things as, "Now we ought to start working on this guy...or on that guy."

Two things happened: first, the crew started doing better work for Geneva Steel; and second, some of the workers started going to church and getting ready to go to the temple.

RUMORS

Rumors started. You might say that what I'd done brought me into disrepute throughout the whole plant. I became known as a religious fanatic from the north gate to the south gate and in between. My nonmember bosses and one of the LDS anti-Church men started getting on my case. I found myself sitting in the office once in a while, kind of being chewed out. But that didn't bother me. I thought I was doing a good thing by getting people to go to church. They were better off going to church than they were drinkin' and smokin'.

You see, there's a federal law. If you're in management, you cannot impose your religion on anybody at work. It's against labor laws. Also, I was embarrassing a lot of people. Still I kept encouraging people to go to church. I also didn't get merit raises. That was because I was a nonconformist, often bending the rules and thus getting myself in trouble.

At the end of a three-month period, each foreman was called in for an evaluation. By then, I was supposed to have written up a dozen evaluation slips on my men, including three reprimands and one suspension—for things they had done wrong. So I knew I was in trouble.

I was demoted from foreman on the furnace down to the labor gang. After three days, I was called to the office and told to write down why I had not written up violation slips and reprimands. If the office didn't like what I had written, I would be fired.

But the Lord always helps you somehow.

The guys at the plant knew I had been demoted and was on the verge of being fired. They called me and said, "Hey, we'll help you somehow." They wanted me to stay—I was now that well liked and respected. I believe that was because of my religious convictions and because I had tried to help *them* when they needed help.

I came home and spent the whole evening writing up why I had not written up reprimands and suspensions. I said it was wrong to punish a man by suspending him because that also punished his wife and kids. I'd taken a psychology course at BYU, so I also tossed in a bunch of fancy terms.

I handed my paper to the superintendent the next morning, a Wednesday. This man had degrees from BYU and some family connections with the university, even though he didn't go to church. He read the letter over, then called me in to his office that afternoon. Three big shots in the office started working me over, telling me I'd better start looking for another job—though I'd not been formally fired yet. The decision would be made on Friday.

The rumors continued to fly among the workers. It happened that on the blast furnace, the company rule was that if a man was absent, the most senior person would fill in if nobody else would take the job. Everybody knew that I was being disciplined because I hadn't written up reprimands on guys who might also have been in trouble.

A coincidence happened which I believe saved my job.

The number 1 man on the blast furnace, the "stove tender," was not LDS, and he had made a mistake on the stoves and just about ruined a furnace. As a result, he was reprimanded right on the spot and sent home for three days. The man who was supposed to move up said, "I'm not movin' up."

The hourly men got together through the union and said to me, "You're the oldest man. You *have* to move up."

"Wait a second," I said. "If I make the same mistake, are you gonna send *me* home and give *me* three days off, just because *he* got three days off?"

"Yes."

"Well," I said, "I'm not doing that. I'll stay where I'm at. I refuse to take the job, because the section on safety in the contract says I'm not usually on the job, so I can't afford to make a mistake. My family will lose three days' pay. I'm refusing that job because of safety. If you want somebody back on that job, you can call the usual guy back. You sent him home, you can call him back."

Now the union men had to go down through seniority.

About then, the shift changed, and I was supposed to go home at four-thirty. No foreman went home, because there might be a walk-out, and if nobody took the job, management would have to run the furnaces.

Every man all the way down to the lowest laborer refused the job, and they were sitting down in the lunchroom. The furnaces were idle. But the furnaces had to be cast. Management couldn't force the men to take the job because of the safety clause in the contract. I hadn't been told to stay, so I went home because I was the one who had been elevated to be fired.

By now, it all boiled down to money, a reprimand, and a man being sent home. So the man who'd been sent home was brought back before the other men would return to the furnaces.

Now the whole plant, that is, the union, was united on one thing: the fate of the man who'd been sent home with a reprimand. Only now, it had become a safety issue, not a violation issue. Management not only had retracted the reprimand but also paid the man for the work he'd missed the night before. Otherwise, the union wouldn't go back to work.

I went to work the next day, Thursday, and nobody said a thing to me.

Friday, I was called to the office, where my fate would be decided. A young foreman, a metallurgist right out of college, was working the midnight shift on his way up through the ranks to become a superintendent in a few years. He was the one giving the orders, handing out the violations. But on the midnight shift, he'd run into some trouble. The casts had been late, the men were dragging their feet, and the work wasn't getting done. The union was pulling kind of a majority slowdown, and management knew it.

I was asked, "Do you know anything about this?"

"No, I don't." But I did—the hourly guys had told me.

"Well look, we're not going to fire you. You go home tonight and come back at midnight on that guy's shift."

The foreman on that shift was reassigned.

So I reported to the midnight shift on the furnaces and was back in the plant's good graces.

But before I went back, I said to the superintendent, "I've thought this over. I really don't want to lose my job. I need my job. I appreciate the chance to go back up to the furnaces, and I'll tell you what. I'll write up four violations and write up a reprimand within three days, to make my quota. This is a good crew to target. You say they're having trouble, so I'll have no problem writing up reprimands."

"We don't want any reprimands," the man explained. "We don't want any violations. We don't want a walkout."

I agreed. I had kind of forced their hand, my way of being proud of what had happened. So I was back on the furnaces.

Then I had to fire a couple of Mexican workers, so they sued me for discrimination—for supposedly preaching on the job, and so forth. A Catholic woman was then fired. She was too small to work on the blast furnaces, and I'd interviewed her about her limitations four or five times. After six months, I had to let her go. The Mexicans went to the U.S. Department of Labor. Now there's a lawsuit against Geneva Steel, and I was the religious preacher and the foreman who'd fired the woman.

After the preliminary hearing, I told the company lawyers, "Don't worry about it. We'll win the case. It will never go to trial. I've followed the book. I've got all the papers from the personal interviews, and the woman has signed them."

The lawyers weren't so sure. Discrimination cases always seemed to go against the company.

At the trial, out came all the accusations.

The judge asked me, "Do you have anything to say?"

"Yes, everything they've said is lies."

"Can you prove that?"

"I'll tell you what, Your Honor, I do not discriminate against Hispanic people or black people or against anybody. When I sent these people up to the furnaces, they felt I owed them a living. They simply didn't perform their work. I'd like to show you the records I kept."

I explained that I had a Hispanic man, also a Catholic, who was the finest man working on the furnace. "If you've got any other Hispanic people like him, I'll take them all. But these men are not that kind.

"Here's what I wrote down about the woman, in my own handwriting. The foreman signed it, and here's her signature. She has a copy of it."

I handed the judge the reports. He looked them over, looked at the woman, and asked her, "Did you get a copy of this report?" and so on.

She said she had.

"Then why are you making all these accusations against this man? Did he ever say anything to you about religion?"

"No, but I once heard him tell a man he was going to hell."

I interjected: "It was to a friend of mine."

The judged looked at me: "Are you religious?"

"I'm probably considered a religious fanatic."

"You know there's a law against promulgating your religion at work."

"Yes, Sir, I know that. And I violate that once in a while. But nobody I've talked religion to has ever registered a complaint about it."

"Well in that case, we have no complaint. And if the accusing parties don't have a complaint, there's no violation. Case dismissed."

The company lawyers bought me a milkshake on the way home. Had Geneva lost the case, it would have cost the company a million dollars. So I was rewarded with a milkshake!

I'd been spared again.

TROUBLE

I got in trouble yet another time because of the Church.

The No. 1 furnace had been shut down for a reline. I'd always been the labor foreman on the relines, but this time I'd been assigned somewhere else. On a reline, the dust catcher (a huge cylinder with a cone on the bottom) has to be cleaned out. Dust collects there over the years, and it becomes hard as a brick. When the furnace is down, workers go down through the manholes on the top to clean the dust catcher out. This time, the catcher was eighty percent full, making the furnace operate inefficiently.

The workers hadn't realized how full the dust catcher was. So all the engineers and superintendents had a meeting to figure out how to clean it out. I'd done that job with laborers and jackhammers, but the leaders decided they'd cut a twelve-inch hole at the bottom, run a cable up through the dust catcher to the manhole, and with cranes and hoists rake the dust out with a bull-nosed I-beam. Some $50,000 dollars was appropriated to do the job.

As I watched the work progress, my thought was, *Oh, boy, this thing's goin' no place. Somebody's goin' to be in trouble.*

The superintendent admitted as much. He knew the job should have been done two weeks before.

This was Friday night, and I had Saturday and Sunday off. But I got a call from the office: "Bones, you've probably heard we're in trouble on this reline, and the problem is the lousy dust catcher. We've just learned that people are coming from Pittsburgh to see how the reline in coming along, and we've already used all our budget for the reline. You've been on the relines before, haven't you?"

"Yes, I've been on relines."

"Would you mind not working your regular job tonight, and go up there to see what you can do about cleaning part of the dust catcher out?"

I told the superintendent, "I'll tell you what I'll do. If you'll let me pick the eight men I want, and guarantee that I can work in the catcher by myself, and not one soul comes to watch me, I'll do it. I don't want anyone there who's in charge of the reline. You just tell everybody that that job is mine. I'll get half the dust out before midnight, and the other half Monday morning, before the Pittsburgh people get here."

The superintendent was skeptical. "We've never had a dust catcher cleaned in that short a time."

"I know that," I admitted, "because you've always had to follow procedures, which are written up by people. I know a way to clean it out without anybody gettin' hurt."

He made some phone calls and made sure everybody was told to stay away from the dust catcher.

I picked the eight men I wanted, all faithful members of the Church, most of them returned missionaries who'd worked with me from time to time. I told them what I wanted them to do. The catcher was eighty feet high and twenty-five feet in diameter—and it was full.

I won't go into the details of how we did it, only to say that we had to work in pairs, on ladders, ropes and safety belts, and with jackhammers. It was dangerous work.

About eight o'clock that evening, the superintendent stuck his head in the manhole to remind me that we hadn't made much progress with our cutting.

I told him, "That's right, but we've still got till midnight." Then I told my guys, "Take forty-five minutes off for lunch."

The superintendent kept insisting I couldn't do the job.

"Listen," I told him, "I'm in charge of this job. Now you're over here spying on us against my rules. Only three people know that these guys are gonna get forty-five minutes. You're one of 'em, I'm one of 'em, and God's not going to tell. So if anybody says anything, it's going to be you. You just get back down to the engineering shack." By then, we'd pretty well had our cuts done with the jackhammers anyway.

He got on my case pretty hard, and I guess I'd been a little hard on him.

We kept cutting, like we were cutting a pie. My men hung down as far as they could on the ladders. Then I told them, "Okay, now we're gonna undercut along the bottom of the cone." Our jackhammers couldn't reach that far, so we got ten-foot hex bars, put them in the eight jackhammers, and vibrated them against the dust catcher wall. The sound was deafening. We were wearing dust masks.

All of a sudden, the whole half of the wall we'd cut went sheeew! It felt like an earthquake, and we were all on ladders, in our safety belts, hanging on to ropes. The dust catcher was clatterin' like the wheels of hell, and dust was falling everywhere.

Now, nobody's saying anything. There's absolute silence while we're waiting for the dust to settle. If we'd taken our masks off, our lungs would have filled up and we'd have been dead men.

The project engineer is now there. I ask him, "How much have we got?"

"It looks like you've got about half of it."

"What time is it?"

"About a quarter after ten."

"Let's see, I have until midnight, don't I?"

"You bet."

My guys were black as coal, so I said to them, "You've done a pretty good job, but you're not supposed to go home till eleven-thirty. Go down, take a long shower, wash your clothes, hang them up to dry, and then go home."

The engineer protested: "You can't let them go home!"

"I don't know why not. I said I'd have half the job done by midnight, and we've been given till Monday morning. My men have earned an early shower, and if any of these guys get in trouble for showerin' early, it's gonna be your fault, 'cuz God's not going to tell the boss, and the boss is not going to get a revelation."

The same eight guys were back on the job by eight o'clock the next morning. The Pittsburgh people would be landing in Salt Lake City at ten, and they wouldn't be at the plant till eleven.

"Tell me," the engineer asked, "how did you get that half out."

"I don't want anyone to know how I did it, because you might say it was against procedures, and I don't want to give all my men reprimands."

"I appreciate that," he said.

By ten-fifteen, we had the other half out. The next week, I was promoted to general foreman.

It was while I was general foreman when I got in the worst trouble of my whole life at Geneva Steel.

An active member of the Church, a metallurgist with a master's degree, came to me and said, "I need to talk to you in private. You're on the afternoon shift. Tomorrow at ten o'clock, you're to be in the front office and see the superintendent of the plant. You're the only man being interviewed tomorrow."

"What for?" I asked.

"I don't know, but I'll try to find out and call you back tonight."

This was when I was a mission representative for the Quorum of the Twelve, visiting missions of the Church. (I'll tell later how that calling came about—again, something of another miracle.)

November 1942. Geneva, Utah. Columbia Steel Co. "Partly finished open hearth furnaces and stacks for a mill which will soon be producing vitally needed steel." Photo by Andreas Feininger.

This man called me that evening. "You're on your own. You're in the worst trouble anybody has ever been in out here. You might be fired tomorrow. I spoke up for you, because you're the best foreman we've got. The superintendent, a Lutheran, thinks you're an excellent man. I'll see you tomorrow afternoon."

I had a sleepless night. I didn't eat any breakfast. I put on a suit and a tie and went to the superintendent's office half an hour early.

The receptionist said to me, "You must be Herschel Pedersen. Oh, I feel sorry for you. You're in big trouble."

"What's going on?"

"This place is full of rumors. Do you know who's here? It's a psychiatrist from Harvard University. He's here to interview you. They think you're crazy."

"They think I'm crazy?!"

"Well, they think there's something wrong with you."

I was taken to the superintendent's office about fifteen minutes early. His secretary said to me, "Everybody in the plant knows about you. Everybody respects you in one way—you've got a reputation for being a good man, a righteous man, able to get work out of your people; but this morning, you're in trouble. The assistant superintendent is with the doctor, and they're talking with the plant superintendent and your boss."

My boss came out and he was red as a beet. He shook my hand, but he didn't say a word. The superintendent said to the psychiatrist, "You're welcome to use my office."

The psychiatrist began: "You know, I've been here for two days. I spent all day yesterday at the Visitors' Center at Temple Square in Salt Lake City, except when I went to lunch. I'm conversing with you because you're a fanatical Mormon. I'd like to ask you some questions about your church."

"I'll admit I'm a fanatical Mormon," I told him.

"How does your church feel about Geneva Steel?"

"My church thinks it's a great place. Look at all the young men who get to go on missions because their dads and moms have good jobs here. Look at the college education it provides young people. Look at the homes it's bought. I see nothing wrong with that."

"You're the highest ranking member of the Mormon Church who works here."

"What do you mean, 'highest ranking'?"

"Don't you have some fancy position in your church?"

"No, I don't have a fancy position. I'm a lay member. I don't get paid nothin'."

"But you go down and visit the missionaries."

(He was referring to my work as a mission representative for the Quorum of the Twelve.)

"That's right, but that's no fancy or high-ranking position. We have bishops, stake presidents, and patriarchs here at the plant—and all of them rank higher than I do. I'm just an elder in my church." (I was a seventy then, but I didn't want to get in a discussion of "seventies.")

We talked about the Church for a while.

Then he asked me, "Would the Church cooperate with you if we had trouble here?"

"I'll tell you what—if you have trouble with these guys, and you think we're having trouble with the union, you just tell me. I'll have the stake presidents invite these guys to a chapel, and I'll talk to them. We'll end the trouble for you. The Church will help you end the trouble."

"Your Church would do that?"

"Yes, we'd be glad to."

"Are all the workers members of your church?"

"No. The Church members pay tithing to the Church—ten percent of their wages. You stop and think: the more people we have working here, the more tithing they pay; and the more chapels and temples we can build. Our church doesn't earn anything more than the tithing we pay. So we'll do anything we can to keep this place going."

"I appreciate that," he said.

Then he started to ask me specific questions, for example, "Why don't you give reprimands out?"

"Well, I'm going to tell you something. You're right, I don't give reprimands out. I don't do a lot of things that maybe I should. In my church, we believe in being forgiving. I believe in being kind. I don't think we should punish a man's family for something he does. There ought to be a more equitable way to punish a man. I don't think a man should get off scot-free if he makes a mistake, but I don't think we should punish the wife and children. I don't think God intends that, and I don't think it's humane."

"Then how do you punish people?"

"I don't punish them. I let the men punish themselves. If a man sooner or later makes a mistake and I punish him, then the other guys sympathize with him, and now you've got everybody against you. You have a contentious crew. They're looking at their foreman, and now they don't respect him. You've got a barrier between management and the union. So let the crew punish the man.

"Let me give you an example. The other day, the crew was casting the furnace, and the first helper lost the gate." (The basin gate holds the iron in, and if the gate is gone, the slag and iron both go into the iron ladle, and you can't have slag in the iron ladle. Iron and slag run all over the floor.) "By rule, the helper should have been given a reprimand and three days off, without pay.

"I said to the men, 'Why don't you guys go take a break and have lunch and a drink? I'll put water on the iron that's on the floor and try to cool it down.

"I didn't say anything to the guilty man. I wet the iron down, got a crane operator to clean it up, and about twenty minutes later I went and said to the men, 'Guys, the iron's all cleaned up.' In about another twenty minutes, we were ready to cast the furnace out.

"The guy who made the mistake knew he was in trouble, so I didn't need to say anything to him. I just asked the whole crew to hurry up, work hard, and get the job done. We had to make another quick cast and get the furnace back on schedule. So they all had to work double because of the mistake.

"Now the crew had been in there thinking, 'What's he going to do to this guy? He should be punished somehow.'

"The next day when I went down to the lunch room, there was the crew, working this guy over, calling him a jerk, a dumb idiot: 'If you lose the gate today, we're going to beat you to death.' None of those guys were gonna make another mistake today.

"That's how the crew takes care of their own. I'm still in good graces with the crew. By the way, I can get more work out of the crew by following that procedure."

After about two hours with the doctor, he said to me, "Well, I see nothing wrong. I think you're a perfectly normal individual."

I thanked him: "I appreciate that." While we were talking I'd thrown in a few words I'd learned from my psychology books: *approach, avoidance, ambivalence,* etc.

"Oh," he said, "you understand those words?"

"Yeah, I took a couple of classes in psychology at BYU."

He gave the bosses a favorable report. The report hadn't been too favorable to start with, but the Lord turned it out different.

If you preach the gospel, the Lord blesses you, even when you get in trouble. As the line in *The Sound of Music* goes, "The Lord never shuts a door but what he opens a window.

MAKING IRON

Something else happened that teaches that same principle—that the Lord never shuts a door but what he opens a window.

We made another kind of iron, called *merchant iron,* coded by numbers and letters. If you know the code, you know what kind of iron it is. The first number indicates the amount of silicon, the second number the amount of manganese, and the third number the amount of phosphorus.

There's another kind of iron that nobody likes to make: *bastard iron,* whose code was F123. Only about forty-five to fifty percent of it ever got made properly, which means when it's made wrong, you have to scrap it and remelt it in the furnace. It's an expensive process.

I was filling in for the "spell" foreman (the general foreman) on the midnight shift, my first time in that position. When I came to work, a note was handed to me: "Make a ladle of F123." My heart about failed me—*Oh, this can't happen to me!* I'd never made a ladle before, though I'd helped the other general foreman do it. But now *I'm* in charge.

The foreman (on the A blower) and I sat down together and reviewed all the chemical composition of the iron for the last twenty-four hours. Soon we were weighing out the manganese and phosphorus—everything had to be right to the pound, because it had to be controlled with a very close tolerance. So it was a pound of this, a pound of that, so much sulfur and so on.

We'd measured everything, but I was uptight. The hoppers were along the iron runner, so we dumped the stuff in the ladle where it was mixed, and then went down to the pig machine. If the pig machine says it's all right, it's shipped.

But as we were putting the silicon in, I realized, "We don't have enough silicon."

The other foreman asked me, "What do you mean, We don't have enough silicon? How much more do we need? We figured it three times."

I hollered to the train operator: "Go get me some silicon!"

"How much?"

"A clam full."

When a clam is dipped into the silicon, it can grab five hundred pounds, or it can grab a ton.

As the clam comes up with silicon, I'm asking myself, *What am I doing?!*

I pull the clam sideways and crack it a little. The silicon empties into the ladle.

The foreman (there'd been some competition between him and me) warned me, "Wait till I tell them in the morning what you did. You'll be fired."

"That's all right!" I fired back.

He looked at me and said, "We've always been friends."

I replied, "I want to be general foreman, and you want to be general foreman. But I've been given this opportunity to spell the general foreman. Why don't you wait till tomorrow night and see the analysis when this batch comes back? If it's right, we'll both take the credit. If it's wrong, I'll tell them I did it. You won't have to take any blame."

"I'll give you that much latitude, and I appreciate your attitude," he said.

I didn't sleep very well that night, and the next day was a bad day. I went to work forty-five minutes early on the midnight shift because I wanted to see if the ladle of iron had had to be scrapped.

There was a note in the general foreman's office: "Congratulations. The iron was perfect. Absolutely perfect!"

When I showed the note to my friend the foreman, he asked me, "How did you come up with the idea of putting the extra silicon in?"

I thought I'd been inspired, but I didn't dare say it. From that point on, I made all that kind of iron for the corporation. I also thanked all the guys who had helped me.

After about two years as general foreman, making this special kind of iron, I learned that the research department from Pennsylvania was going to come out to the plant. Geneva was making that iron and shipping it clear to Virginia, or clear up to Canada, but the Pennsylvania plane was just thirty miles from the shipping destination. U.S. Steel was needlessly spending thousands of dollars in freight.

The lab research crew and the scientists came out to observe me making iron. By this time I had everything memorized. The research people were looking at all the casts, their calculators in their hands, asking how much of this I was going to put in, how much of that. "Well, aren't you going to figure it out?" they asked me.

"No, if that's what it is, we've got to raise it ten points. You've got the charts, don't you? Doesn't the chart say…?"

"Well, yeah," one of the men said.

"Then why do I have to sit and write it all down? I already know what the chart says."

They realized that I knew all the charts and what to put in the cast. The iron's running down into the furnace, and I'm telling the guy how much of what to put in. All the scientists are checking each other—"We've got to be scientific," they're saying.

They spent the entire week watching me make iron, and then they wrote up a big report for the corporation. Now they were going to teach another plant how to make iron. Geneva didn't have to make that kind anymore.

The report concluded, "After all the calculations, and all the computations and figures, there's a certain feeling that every man has to learn on his own, because the analysis changes as it comes from the furnace. And a man learns that by a certain gut feeling."

I replaced the general foreman, and he was a great guy. We worked together five days a week. But because I was a religious fanatic, he was always belittlin' me and cussin'. One day he said to me, "You know, I respect you and the Mormon religion. My wife goes to church all the time, but I can never be active in this church because of what some of the bishops I've known have done."

I myself could tell lots of stories about Church leaders who had stolen things at Geneva, but that's not the point. This man would not go to church, he claimed, because of what he knew about bishops, but he always respected me. Still, whenever I talked to someone about the Church, he'd belittle the Church.

Every once in a while, I'd be able to slip in a positive sentence or two about the Church, and that went on between him and me for years. The day he retired, I got his job as general foreman.

I didn't hear from him, though I knew he lived in Spanish Fork. Two or three years went by, and one day I got a telephone call from

1943. BYU Library: L. Tom Perry Collections: Geneva Steel Photographs and Negatives.

him. "You know," he said, "I've been to the temple, and a lot of that had to do with you. I'm in this ward down here, and the ward is talking about having someone come down and talk about getting people to come back to church. I told 'em that I knew a guy at Geneva who did a lot of that. I'd worked with him. The bishop has asked me to invite you down to speak."

"Well, I'd be glad to do that."

When I arrived at the chapel, ol' So-and-so was standing on the steps in front of the chapel. He came down five or six steps, a big grin on his face. "Boy, am I glad to see you. My wife and I went to the temple within five months of me retiring from Geneva."

"That's great!" I told him.

"I want to thank you for all those little things you kept saying to me. When I said something bad about the Church, you'd say that someday I'd be forgiven. When I cussed those bishops out, you said, 'Well, they're going to hell for what they do. You don't have to worry about them. You're going to be judged for what *you* do. Let the Lord worry about the bishops.' You just said little things like that. Now let's go to the bishop's office. You're on the program today."

I thought it was pretty good of him to take me to meet the bishop.

I looked around the office. Everybody was there, but nobody was sitting in the bishop's chair. *Maybe the bishop's out in the hall, or somewhere,* I thought. Then this fellow went over and sat in the bishop's chair. "I'm bishop of this ward," he announced, "and proud of it."

SWEARING

On the blast furnaces, when the iron comes up out of the tapping hole, it's on a 26 degree angle, and under anywhere from 25 to 33 pounds of pressure; it comes out from a big spigot, 2700 degrees F. hot. So that it doesn't splash all over, there's a splasher plate, so that when the iron hits the plate, it stays in a trough that leads to the runners. When all the iron has left the hole, nothing but hot sparks and slag come out, mostly hot air at 2700 degrees.

Then the splasher plate has to be raised on its hinge. But if the plate doesn't have the proper sand, or a brick falls out of the splasher plate, or a hinge burns off, there's a lot of trouble.

One particular day, on the first cast during the day shift, the splasher plate fell off its hinge and into the trough. This means that the mud gun couldn't get into the hold, and production would be lost. The wind is reduced to only pounds of pressure, and the open hole exposes the molten slag and iron. Sparks and coke are flying from the open hole. It's all a very dangerous situation.

That day, two or three men were trying to hook a cable to the plate and drag it out of the way. The problem was that the men working on the heavy lifting pin, a bar about two and a half inches in diameter and four feet long, became exhausted, because of the intense heat.

I went up and down the other side of the trough with an eight-foot cable, with an eye on the end, in an attempt to pull the pin out, and slide the loop through the holes on the casting. I'd been working on it for five or six minutes, but because of the heat, I too became exhausted. Also, there's only room for two men to work in that space.

Now I'm getting frustrated and perturbed—the three men and I are all exhausted, and there are no fresh bodies around. I said, "Damn it, won't one of you men come help me?"

One of them stepped forward, and I was able to put the pin down, pull it back, and slip the cable over on the first try; we were able to slip the pin through the eye of the cable, and it was just a matter of stretching the cable out and hooking the chain fall onto the monorail crane.

The chain is capable of lifting twenty to thirty tons, so it was just a matter of pulling on the chain fall until it pulled the splasher out of the way. By then, people had cooled down.

That afternoon, I had to go over to cast No. 2 furnace, and as I was walking across what we called the stove deck, a man came up to me. This was a man who smoked, drank, gambled, and by his own admission was immoral—he'd been divorced three or four times. He came up to me and said, "Is what I heard about you true?"

"What did you hear?" I asked him.

"I heard you used the GD word today."

"No, I've never done that."

"When the splasher was stuck and you couldn't get it out, what *did* you say?"

"Well, I got mad and hollered at the guys—'Dammit, won't one of you come over and help me?!'"

"You can't do that."

"I can't say dammit? I've said it many times in my life."

"Out here, everybody looks at you. Everybody measures the Church by you. You're the one we look to. Now if I'd said that, nobody'd have paid attention, but when you say it, it goes all through the department. It didn't take more than fifteen minutes."

I apologized: "I'm sorry. You'll never hear me say that again."

Whenever you're trying to do something for the Church, or to get people to become active in the Church, you're held to a different standard. They may not live the gospel, but they sure do hold you to it. If you don't hold to it, you're considered a hypocrite.

Over my years at the plant, I didn't keep track of how many people we went to the temple with, but one winter my wife and I went to the temple every week with somebody who had been inactive, and now they were going to be sealed and have their children sealed to them. We'd go to the Salt Lake Temple or the Manti Temple, because there was no Provo Temple then.

That was the only time my wife ever saw those people, but she was a great help to me. A man at work was having a bad night, and he was messing up terrible. Everything was going wrong for him. I said to him, "What's the matter? You've never been this poor of a worker."

"Right, I'm in bad trouble. My wife's got cancer, and I don't think she's gonna live. As soon as I get home from work, I've got to take her over to Utah Valley Hospital."

I asked him, "What time do you have to have her there?"

"By ten o'clock."

"Well, I'll tell you what you do. You're through working for tonight, but don't go home, because you'll have to punch yourself out after the shift, or you'll lose your money. I'll get someone to take care of your job for you. You go over there and try to sleep." I told him a place to go sleep.

I got a man to fill in for him, and then at five o'clock in the morning, I called my wife: "Dear, I'm asking you to do me a favor. I know it's five in the morning and you've got a big family there, but the kids will all be going to school. As soon as I get home from work, I'd like to have some fresh-baked bread and some pies. I'd like to take them to so-and-so and his family in Springville before he goes to the hospital."

It was wintertime, a very cold morning, but my wife had all the bread and pies baked, and we took them down to Springville. (These are the kinds of things Shirley was willing to do.)

THE MOVE

A young man and his wife had all kinds of troubles with parents, friends, work, and housing. They decided to just get away and start over in a new place, so they sold what they could, loaded their two children into the car, along with a few possessions, and started driving up the I-15 Interstate. They had saved a few thousand dollars to enable them to start over wherever they found employment.

As they came to each community, the husband tried to find work, but there was none available. Eventually they entered Utah Valley and a few days later happened to drive by the Geneva Steel plant. They saw the sign for employment application. The husband stopped, he was interviewed, and he was told he could start work the next day. The plant had just been authorized to start hiring men to cover summer vacations.

Think what you will, but he began working for me that first day. As we became acquainted, I observed him and learned much about him. He and his wife did not drink, smoke or gamble, and they believed in God, though they never attended any church.

I often worked with him on difficult assignments, and one day when we were alone, I asked him, "Why do you think you ended up working here?"

He replied that he had never thought of that other than that it was a good job.

I told him I believed that God had brought him to Utah Valley for a purpose.

"What purpose could that be?" he asked.

I told him it was to join the Church and save all his deceased ancestors.

Over the next few months, I said nothing to him about the Church except when he asked questions. I answered those questions simply, adding little.

Then I thought it time to say something more specific, since he was to be assigned to a station job as an operator for men on vacations. I would see less of him. So I told him he needed to receive a revelation about the things we had talked about. But he should never join any church unless he and his wife received a witness from the Holy Ghost.

I gave him a Book of Mormon, asked him to read it when he felt inclined to, and let him know that I would never ask him if he was reading it or intended to read it.

A few months went by, during which I never mentioned the Church.

Then on a midnight shift, he called me and asked if I might come to see him at his station job that night. He was crying while explaining that he had read about half of the Book of Mormon—but his wife had read more. They had experienced something unusual. He stated simply that they knew the book to be true and they were ready to join the Church.

I worked for months at Geneva Steel with a number of inactive fellows who later all became active and took their families to the temple. My wife accompanied me to these sealings in the temple, even though she had never met any of the wives or children of these men. About a month before one of these families was scheduled to go to the temple, I received a letter from their seventeen-year-old daughter. She wrote that her father had for months come home from work and told the family everything I had taught him. She thanked me for what I had done to motivate him to take the family to the temple. She wrote how she had taken her younger brothers and sisters to church meetings and encouraged them to pray that their parents would take them to the temple. Both sets of grandparents had also so prayed from the time the couple married.

We arrived at the Manti Temple on a beautiful, cool spring morning before the sun rose. As we got out of the car, the family and grandparents were also arriving. As I turned to greet the children, the seventeen-year-old daughter walked up to me, smiling a broad, beautiful smile. Then she began to cry. She put both arms around my neck and gave me a huge hug.

I was somewhat taken aback, hardly expecting something like that would happen. She let me go, then looked me straight in the face and said, "Meeting you is the greatest thing that has ever happened in our family, or to me."

I was being honored and respected undeservedly. I explained to her that I was nothing but a family friend who worked with her father. All thanks should be given to God, the worker of such miracles.

Consider, readers, all that had brought about this success. Nothing in this life could be more sacred, virtuous or beautiful than the many prayers and efforts of a seventeen-year-old taking her siblings to church and asking them to pray that their parents would take them to the temple. Or how about the many hours and prayers and much fasting by the grandparents in behalf of their children and grandchildren? Those efforts were as sacred as the temple itself. Do these people not deserve more credit, honor or recognition for their many years of hope and patience, their dependence on the Lord than I, who had been but an instrument to bring their efforts to fruition?

One day a young kid just out of high school came up to work on the furnace, and we got to be friendly. He wasn't going to church, and he was dating a girl from Orem High School. I got to talking to him about going on a mission, but he said he didn't want to go on a mission. He was "in love."

He got so he'd come over to the house and we'd go fishing. Then one night he called and said, "I've got to come over and talk to you, and I'm bringing my girlfriend."

When he arrived, I said to him, "I know why you've come."

"Why?"

"The two of you have been immoral, and now you've got to go see your bishop, and you won't be able to go on a mission."

"That's right."

"Could I make a suggestion? Why did the two of you put yourself in this situation?"

My wife and I had once had a talk with Harold B. Lee, who told me, "When I interview a young man and he's been immoral only once, with one girl, I tell him to go home, marry that girl, and not go on a mission."

I said to the boy, "Why don't you go to church and prepare yourself to get married in the temple. But you'll have to talk with your bishop."

"I don't want to talk to my bishop. He'll probably excommunicate me."

I explained, "I'll tell you what I'll do. I will go with you to church on Sunday. All four of us will go—you and your girlfriend, me and my wife. I'll tell the bishop that you've talked to me and that I've brought you to see him. Then we'll go to your girlfriend's sacrament meeting."

I called both bishops and we went to see the boy's bishop: "Bishop," I said, "this boy was going to go on a mission, and he and his girlfriend have been immoral. I've told him he ought to prepare himself to marry this girl in the temple and not go on a mission. He's put himself before you, so you be the judge. I'll step out. If you want the girl to stay here with her boyfriend, that's fine. But I should not be here."

The girlfriend and I stepped out while the bishop talked to the young man. What the young man said, the bishop never did say.

Then I took the young girl over to her bishop, and we did the same thing. After both the couple had talked to their bishops, I said to them, "Now you've got to be morally clean. You can't go on dates alone. You don't go anywhere unless me and my wife or others go with you."

So we dated with them, as did others, and they later married in the Manti Temple, and we were the honored guests.

Six months later, the young man was killed in a car wreck, and his pregnant wife became a widow. About three years later, she remarried, civilly, to another man, and she's raised the children.

But you see, my wife was willing to put herself out and give of her time. We even went out with them at Christmas. If somebody at Geneva was sick or something, we'd take our kids and go sing to them.

THE GREAT FREEZE

One winter was a very severe winter, and everything was freezing up at Geneva. I was on No. 1 blast furnace at the time. I'd been at the ore yard and sinter plant for a lot of years, and at the time, the manager down there passed out all kinds of reprimands and violations. He was generally disliked by everybody down there, even by the faithful Church members. This man himself was serving on a high council.

When everything froze up, you couldn't get any material up to the sinter plant or the screening station to run the blast furnaces, so they weren't operating. In fact, they'd been banked, operating at only five or ten percent of capacity because everything was frozen up.

The company contract says that the company can require people to work overtime in cases of emergency, and when the blast furnace isn't operating, it costs something like three to four thousand dollars every minute—that's what you're losing in production. If nothing's being made in the blast furnace, the open hearth and rolling mills have to be shut down. So you figure that some six thousand people at Geneva are still being paid, and you're looking at millions of dollars being lost everyday because of the cold.

So everybody's being forced to work sixteen hours a day for three days. The daytime temperature is at 11 below zero, and at night, it's 23 below. I'd been working on the furnace on day shift, but nothing was turning. The foremen at the ore yard and the sinter plant had been working overtime, but nothing was going there either. You couldn't get the men to work, they were exhausted and cold, the belts were frozen up, and everything else was going wrong.

This superintendent asked me, "Would you go down there and give 'em a hand for the next few days? We'll have somebody cover the furnace, but you've worked down there, so you know everything."

"I'd be glad to go down," I said.

I pulled on an extra wool shirt—no matter how cold things are, if you work you're going to be warm.

With trouble like that, I always worked *with* the men, even though the contract said I didn't have to. If I'd been someone else, the Union would have filed a grievance against them for not working.

Everybody was in the office at the sinter plant, sitting around talking, explaining to me where the bottlenecks were, and that one belt in particular was frozen up. The men wouldn't work because of the bitter cold. The frozen belt was the difficult challenge. Fires are lighted with diesel fuel and straw to keep the belts thawed out on the head pulleys, but the fire also melts some of the ore, which accumulates and has to be shoveled off. I took thirty men out, but they couldn't get the belt to start.

While sitting around, they talked about wanting to reprimand people and send 'em home—they were going to get tough.

I said to them, "Look, you guys have all been here for a while. I'll tell you what you do—you call the furnaces and tell 'em we'll have ore comin' up there in thirty-five minutes."

"What do you mean?!"

"Well," I explained, "if it's only that one belt that's holding things up, I'll go get those thirty men taking a coffee break. I'll go out and talk to them, and in thirty-five minutes you'll hear the tinkle of rocks comin' across the screens. You just tell them some rocks will be goin' up to the furnace."

"How much?" the foreman asked.

"We'll keep it going all night. We can run three times as much as the furnaces can use, if we don't have to clean the screens."

The foreman challenged me: "Who do you think you are, that you can get these men to work any harder? We've already had 'em out there."

"I didn't say I could get them to work any harder, I just said that the ore would be comin'."

When I went out, all these guys sittin' around looked up at me: "What did they send you down here for? Just 'cuz we like you, you think we're gonna work any harder for you? We're tired of being forced to work overtime, and everything else."

"Well, they're talking about reprimandin' you," I told them. "They're forcing you to stay overtime, aren't they? Look at it this way, guys: They're not the guys that messed you up."

"They're not?"

"It's the Lord who's shut you out of business. He's the one who brought the frost. These guys in the furnaces don't know anything about the frost. You guys are all priesthood holders. We're gonna' go out there now and tell the Lord we've gotta get this belt going. We're gonna get ore coming up to the furnaces. As soon as we get this belt goin', we'll send you guys home, and you won't have to stay all night."

They all looked at me and started to laugh. They were now all happy, even jovial. With picks and jackhammers and sledgehammers and bars, they went to work. I told them not to throw the frozen ore on the belt, just throw it aside. We'd clean it up another day when the weather broke. It was piled up about eighteen to twenty inches, but the jackhammers could break it up. The frozen pieces were thrown to the side.

It was all a mess, and you had to either trip over it or walk around it, but it wasn't stopping the belt any longer. The belt started, the reclaimer was a goin', and the ore started goin' up and around. We threw diesel fuel all over the new bales of straw and lit them (today, you'd be arrested for pollution). The ore piles got hot, and by three o'clock in the morning, all the guys got to go home.

You see, the Lord blesses you.

One time the guys were on kind of a slowdown putting a skimmer in, and the furnace had been delayed two hours. I went over and said to them, "Guys, this furnace has got to be cast." The foreman was there trying to drive them. I said to him, "Why don't you go in and have a coffee break."

Fifteen minutes later, we had the job done that they had been dragging their feet on. The guys knew that I cared about them.

Another time, a guy came up to me and explained a little problem over on the high line. I helped him with it but told him, "You're gonna owe me one day. Someday I'm gonna need your help."

A few days later, I did have a little bit of a problem, and most of the crew knew about it. It had to do with a hot sinter coming out of the sinter plant, so hot it couldn't be drawn into the furnace. The crew would not be able to change the furnace and make any iron. I had refused to give them a reprimand because the stuff wasn't going into the furnace fast enough.

The guys all said, "We're going to get Bones out of trouble." One of them called up the superintendent on the loudspeaker and asked, "Superintendent, are you there?"

"You bet."

"This is So-and-so, and I'm on scale car No. 3. If you don't do something about this blankety-blank thing, we're all going home."

Everybody in the department could hear it. The gripe was based on safety; and on safety, you can go home, with pay.

As the foreman, I said to the guy who had made the announcement, "What's the matter with you?"

"Oh, were gonna' get you out of trouble."

"You're getting me out of trouble? No, you're getting me *in* trouble."

He reassured me, "You don't know the half of it. I'll have everybody over here in a minute. Don't you worry."

So here come the superintendents and everybody, running all over the high line, while all the guys were stirring everything up—they were all going to leave, because it was a safety item. But because it was a safety item, the whole situation changed, and I was out of trouble. The furnace was going again.

GAMBLING PREACHER

At work at Geneva Steel, I was called the "gambling preacher," because I would bet on BYU ballgames. Many of the people I worked with were antagonistic toward BYU, so the bet would be ice cream or watermelon for the crew in the summer, or a steak fry or turkey in the wintertime. (We'd bury the steaks or turkey in the sand, cast hot iron over the meat, let it cook, and then dig it up and eat it. (A turkey cooked that way tastes very good.) It was my way of getting through to the men.

One time BYU was playing New Mexico in football, and I had season tickets. I was working that day so I couldn't go, so the guys asked me, "Who are you betting on?" The newspaper had announced that BYU was favored by 21 points.

"I always favor BYU."

"Well, we'll take New Mexico, and it seems like you always win, so 21 points is not a wide enough margin."

"That's because I got the right on my side." We'd make jokes like that. "But I'll give you 28 points."

They argued for 35, so I said, "Then I'll give you 35 points."

"Will you give us more?"

"Well, all right. I'll be a gentleman and give you 45 points for this game."

I came home and told my wife that I was going to have to buy ice cream, because I'd spotted BYU by 45 points.

Everybody at work had the radio on, and BYU won by 45 points. I said to the guys, "What kind of ice cream do you want?" That's the kind of thing I did all the time.

There was always an undertone of objections that I preached too much and so didn't get a lot of promotions. Nobody said anything to me about it, especially after I won the lawsuit about ten years before I retired.

I'd been the tear-down foreman on the blast furnace before I became general foreman. The guys who worked under me on tear-down would use jackhammers to loosen the brick in the furnaces, and those jackhammers weighed 110 pounds. As many as twenty-five jackhammers might be working in the furnace in one night.

On graveyard shift, everybody would be asleep while I would be standing on a scaffold, while thousands of tons of bricks would be falling down. I would sometimes pick up a jackhammer, tell a worker to take a break for a minute, and then I'd go to work. So ninety percent of the time, I would be on the jackhammer and the crew would be running the tear-down.

If there was a hard job to do, I'd help out. That's why the guys would work harder for me than they would for other foremen. I could tear a furnace down faster than anybody else.

One night, we were jackhammering out the bottom of the furnace so the big hearth staves could be removed—they weighed about twenty to thirty tons each, were about eight feet high, eight to ten inches thick, and about 6 feet wide with circulating water running through the pipes to cool the hearth. The boilermakers and millwrights were unable to move them as they were in so tight. My men had to get them out. They'd been working two days on the job but couldn't get the job done.

The superintendent asked me, "Can you get those hearth staves out?"

"You bet I can," I said, "in twenty minutes," all the while knowing that they were wedged in, and the crew was having trouble burning them out with torches.

"How will you do that?"

The superintendent told the construction engineer to leave the hearth staves alone and take his crew on to something else. "Bones will get them out in twenty minutes."

You see, superintendents believe in you. They have faith in you.

On the furnaces, we burned the tapping hole with a drill, down about six to nine feet. The rest of the foot or foot-and-a-half was hard as a brick, so we had to drill down farther. We threw some coal to the bottom of the tapping hole, then lit an oxygen lance—which is pure oxygen. Oxygen will burn through just about anything at that high temperature. I would use the oxygen lance to burn the hearth staves.

I hooked an oxygen hose from the No. 2 furnace and told the guy with the torch to light me off one of the steel pipes. He cracked the oxygen a little, put the torch up, and the pipe started to burn. I put that in the copper hearth stave, and I could see the steel melting in a little pool of copper. "Okay," I said, "turn it up a little more."

In about fifteen or twenty minutes, I had a little hole of molten iron. I hollered, "Turn her all the way up!" I fed the steel pipe straight down through the copper stave.

The pipe fitters hooked up five more pipes and fed me just enough pipe to burn the iron. The pipes were burning and flying all over. In twenty minutes, the hearth stave popped right off the wall.

After you've done a few things like that, the superintendents trust you.

MY FRIEND

One of our friends, a man I'd worked with (he hadn't been a one hundred per center when it came to church), when he became a bishop, invited me to speak in his ward. When he introduced me, he said, "This is the only man on the face of the earth who could tell me to go to hell, and I would love him for saying it." I guess that's how much he loved me.

Very few people I worked with failed to become active Church members after only two or three visits with them. They might start coming to church, but it's after you become friendly with them and visit with them over a period of time, a year or two, they come to the point where they will accept and believe just about anything you say if you show them in the scriptures. I was always there for them, even in the middle of the night, whatever the matter was.

I worked with one inactive Church member at Geneva who'd gambled, smoked, drank, stepped out on his wife, wrecked his car—just about everything bad you could do. He had a wife and a bunch of kids. I'd go to his home in Springville, and his wife would say to me, "You know, when he's trying to quit smoking, it's the worst thing in the world. I'd rather have him smoke than be that way. I'd rather have him never go to church than be the way he is when he tries to stop smoking. We can't stand him in the family anymore."

I told her, "We've got to do some fasting and praying for him. We've got to get God to help him."

She agreed.

"Any time you need some help, you just give me a call. I'll be glad to come to your home."

"Okay," she said, "but it might be in the middle of the night.

"Whenever it is, it won't bother me."

One night this man and I were on swing shift, and he'd been having a rough time. All the other guys were smoking, and he wasn't. I said to him, "Hang in there. Let's have a little prayer, and the Lord will help you."

About two o'clock that morning, the phone rang, and it was his wife. "You said to call. My husband's throwing a nicotine fit. He says he can't sleep, and he's got all the family awake. Please come down here."

"I'll be right there."

So away I went, whipping down the highway at two o'clock in the morning. When I walked into the home, the whole family were ripping on this man, and he was ripping on them.

I'd been working with this man for many years. I'd been fishing with him. I knew his wife. I knew his kids. I knew I could say anything to him—people can have that kind of faith in somebody. "Look," I said, "I can't stop you from smoking. I can't remove your desire for a cigarette. But I'm your friend, and I'm here. Right now, there's no peace in the family. Why don't we all kneel and have a family prayer?

"Sir, why don't you ask God to help you in this matter?"

Then I asked the wife to offer a little prayer—which she did.

"Now I'll offer a prayer."

I gave the husband a blessing and said, "It's late. You go in to bed. You've had your family up and all disrupted. The kids have to go to school in the morning."

I turned to the wife: "When you get up in the morning, have family prayer, and then fix a nice breakfast for your husband, just like it was your wedding day."

Again to the husband: "And when you get up in the morning, you pray and tell God that if he'll help you through this, you'll never mess up on anything again...and you'll never want a cigarette again."

When he came to work the next morning, I asked him, 'How did it go last night?"

"We slept till ten o'clock in the morning—the whole family. The kids didn't go to school. We had bacon, eggs and pancakes for breakfast."

He never had any trouble with smoking again—never! The point is that when you've known a person that long, you can say anything you want to him.

Another time, a general foreman in his sixties at Geneva Steel had never been married in the Church, he'd never held any priesthood, even though one of his sons was a bishop. One day when I was to relieve him, he was up in the office on the furnace, where everybody was knocking the Church down about tithing and other things. That kind of got to me, and I can be a little aggressive at times. I said to the guys, "You don't pay tithing, but someday you're going to wish you had."

I said to the inactive fellow, "Look at it this way—you don't pay tithing, but you've got a son who's a bishop."

"That's right," he admitted.

I knew this man had been very frugal (he was probably worth about half a million dollars). "All that money you've got in the bank, all your stocks, yet you've never paid any tithing in your life. When you die, what's going to happen to your house and other belongings—your boats, your Oldsmobile, your money?"

"My son's going to—"

"That's right. The Church is going to get your tithing anyway, because as a bishop, he's going to tithe what you leave him. So you can pay now, or we'll get it when you're dead. It doesn't matter either way—we're going to get your money."

He admitted, "I think what you're saying is right."

I just say things like that, I guess, because I have the moral authority to do it. And I don't bend what I say.

Work at Geneva wasn't too hard, but after I'd been there six or eight years, I talked to Alma Burton about teaching seminary. He said the program would be glad to have me—my reputation for getting guys to come to church had spread among the local bishops. Some of them would say to me, "So-and-so has started to come to church. Why don't you come and talk at my ward?"

But I was making pretty good money at Geneva, saving for my children's missions and education. Had I started to teach seminary, I could never have afforded that.

Work in the blast furnace was considered the first or second worst job at the plant, depending on who you talked to. But I loved my work, and I fully expected that I would be made general foreman of the three blast furnaces. I was over a lot of men—all the men on the furnaces, the high lines, the center flats, the ore yards, dumping crews, and the pig machines. That gave me some increase in salary, but not a great increase.

I worked all shifts—days, swing, graveyard. When I was on graveyard or swing, I'd come home and never miss meetings, no matter the time of the day they were held, but of course I missed meetings if I was on day shift. I'd get four Sundays off every sixteen weeks.

Talk about experiences, shift work became one of the great experiences of my life, and I believe it shows how the Lord works.

Chapter Ten

High Council-Missionaries

Elder Boyd Packer, while visiting our stake conference, suggested to the stake president that I be put on the high council, assigned to work with the young men and women of missionary age who were taking drugs, drinking, being immoral, or doing other wayward things. So I became a "hippie" home teacher.

My wife laughed at my calling, but I began visiting the young men and women once a month. Six months later, there had been no progress. I said to my wife, "The best thing we can do for these kids is to kill them all and then do their work in the temple." She reminded me that that was not an option.

A verse in the D&C (105:37) came to my mind: "And inasmuch as they follow the counsel which they receive, they shall have power after many days to accomplish all things pertaining to Zion." If we do what we are called to do and remain faithful, the Lord will fulfill his promises. Then I got my first break.

Jack was smoking marijuana, drinking, and living in an apartment by Salt Lake Community College, having been kicked out of his home by his parents. So I would go to Salt Lake to visit him; then I would have him visit with his parents, trying to get them back together. One day he surprised me by telling me he would be willing to change and go on a mission. Can you imagine my excitement after six or eight months of no success?

His parents allowed him to move back home. He began attending church and finally did go on a mission, but he had to have an interview with a General Authority. It took two years to get him on his mission. After his return, he served as a bishop, twice on the high council, and now he has his own business with several employees. He was my first!

As I visited these boys and girls I realized I needed to visit with them twice a month. I was on the afternoon shift, so I would begin visiting at 8:30 in the morning. (You could always catch them home because they were in bed recovering from the night before.) I visited until about 1:30, went home, ate and then went to work. On the graveyard shift, I would get home about 7:30, have breakfast, and then go visit until 1:30 in the afternoon. On day shift, I would visit from about 6:30 until 9:00 at night.

As the work progressed, the stake president gave me three assistants: Dennis Daniels, Richard Magelby and Donald Fowler. From that time forward, at least two of us always made visits together.

One of our greatest successes happened to be a young man who had been on drugs for three years. He had moved to American Fork from California after the death of his father in an airplane accident. Losing their business and moving to American Fork was a traumatic experience for the entire family. The young man became inactive, used drugs and alcohol, and was immoral. He ended up living in an apartment with another guy and a girl they both shared. As I visited with him, he had no interest in going to Church, no interest in a mission. I told him someday the Lord would get his attention.

As fate would have it, in the month of January on an extremely cold night, he and the girl friend decided to get married. When the other roommate came home, they informed him that there would be no more sex with him, and he had to move out. The roommate left, but when he returned, he had a shotgun. He forced the couple into the shower with their clothes on. Then he took them out to the car, drove up Tibble Fork Dam in American Fork Canyon, made them get out of the car, and tied them together, back-to-back, with telephone wire. Then he drove down the canyon, leaving them there with no coats and in wet clothes. The roommate hit this young man over the head with a pipe, an injury that eventually required 123 stitches.

Somehow they managed to get loose and survived a five-mile trek down the canyon to where they knocked on someone's door. The family took them to the hospital.

This young man, now ready to listen, said he was willing to change his life and move back home. But his brothers and sisters said they didn't want him there. He was a disgrace to the family. His mother loved him and allowed him to move back in.

We were now visiting him every week. Things were extremely difficult at home. One night he came home very late, gathered all the sheets off his bed and his underclothing, and dyed them black. His mother called to tell me she couldn't take it anymore. She was going to kick him out. His bishop, a highway patrolman, lived right across the street from him. I called his bishop and asked him to take Dwight for a ride for an hour while I talked with his mother.

I talked with the mother and told her the only thing wrong with her son was that he had had an experience with witchcraft that night. Over the visits he had told me about some of his friends who were involved with witchcraft.

His mother finally agreed to let him stay in the house for another month, and now we are visiting him twice a week because of the tension in the house. He was now also attending all church meetings. In a few months, the bishop called him to teach Primary, and he became a very good Primary teacher. Now he was asking me about how long it would be before he could go on a mission. I told him it might take two years.

He happened to be a very intelligent young man. He got a very good job and saved all his money. After a couple of years, he was called to be the welfare secretary for the elders quorum, while still teaching Primary.

The Brethren still didn't feel good about his going on a mission. He was very disappointed; he thought two years should be enough for repentance. We continued to visit, encouraged him, and he became a devoted reader of the scriptures, though beginning to lose all hope of ever going on a mission. He was now twenty-five years old.

The first fast meeting of the new year, a woman thanked the elders quorum for helping her pay her delinquent light bill. Then the elders quorum president set the record straight: the elders quorum hadn't done anything; it was this young man. Because he couldn't go on a mission, at least he could help the poor.

At age twenty-six, he finally received a mission call to Denmark. He has been faithful in the Church ever since.

Another young man who moved to American Fork from Arizona with his family loved to sing in choirs. Somehow in the move, this young man had got lost in the shuffle and gone inactive. Despite being an A student in high school, he was now a dropout. He even got kicked out of his home and was living in Orem.

When I first went to visit his parents, they expressed no hope for him. I asked them if it was all right if I had their son come back to their home so we could all visit together. They agreed.

The first visit wasn't too good. As I talked to the parents, they were unwilling to compromise in any way. So the son and I met two or three times with the parents. Then I met with the parents alone to tell them there had to be some form of compromise or there would be no hope for their son.

After a few compromises, the young man moved back home and began coming to church. It was very difficult for them and for him, but as time went by, he finally qualified to go on a mission. When he returned from his mission, BYU would not let him into school. This hurt me more than anything. I wrote a letter to President Wilkinson recommending the young man be admitted to BYU because he had the ability to be a good student, in spite of his past. They still wouldn't let him in. So he went to Arizona State, where he graduated with a master's degree in chemical engineering.

I never heard anymore about him until 1989 when I was mission president in New Zealand. One day there was a letter on my desk from the mayor of Thousand Oaks, California. I wondered why he would be writing to me. The letter asked if I would be willing to write a letter about what I knew about this young man, who had been selected as the most outstanding citizen of the year of Thousand Oaks. At the time, he was also serving as a bishop in the church. I was more than delighted to write a letter, leaving out all the bad things, of course. He eventually moved to Tennessee, where he became an executive, and today he lives in Utah. Recently, when I was performing a sealing, a strange man, a lawyer, introduced himself to me. He said, "I need to tell you thank you from So-and-so. I'm his uncle." He said he was supposed to tell me that I had done more for him (the young man) than any man on the face of the earth.

One young man, a hippie, wandered around the U.S. I called his mother, who I had known when I taught Gleaners in American Fork. I asked her when I could talk to her son. She said that he would be home in the winter because it was too cold to stay away. I asked her to call me when he came home.

She returned my call, and when I went to see him, he was about as big a mess as you could find a young man in. I visited him two or three times, but my visits had no effect. He began avoiding my visits in the evening, so I called his mother and asked her to call me when he was home late at night, so I knew he would be home in the morning. Then I could go visit him.

I had a set of pictures, a study of a young man going from good to bad in seven pictures. I went over at 8:30 in the morning, after graveyard shift. His mother said he was in bed, so I went in and woke him up. He smelled terrible. I said to him, "Do you know there is a war going on?"

He said, "No."

"The war that is going on is between Satan and the Lord. Now it is time you got active in the Lord's army. If you are going to volunteer for one of the armies, which one are you going to join?" He said he would join the Lord's army. I showed him the worst of my pictures. "This is the way Satan's army looks. It looks just like you. You are in the wrong army." Then I showed him all seven pictures, the first of which looked like a missionary in a shirt and tie.

I asked him how long it was going to take for him to enlist in the Lord's army. "You've got all winter before you leave home again. I will come visit you two or three times a week, and I will expect you to be in the Lord's army by spring."

It was a miracle to see the change that took place in the young man. He changed his habits, cut his hair, shaved off his beard and started attending church in a suit and tie.

The great conclusion to this story is the quote by James (5:20): "He which converteth the sinner from the error of his way shall save a soul from death, and shall hide a multitude of sins." Today this young man lives in Connecticut, a fine, upstanding citizen.

Chapter Eleven

Missionary Work

Being a stake missionary family, we also knew of all the poor people in the community. One poor couple lived in a chicken coop, and they were the poorest family I ever knew. They used to go down to the boat harbor and fish for catfish. George Hatch, also a stake missionary, would go down there and befriend them while talking fishing.

I said to George, "We've got to get this man baptized, but he has a sign on his door, 'No Mormons Allowed.'" (The man's wife was a Church member.) "Why don't we talk to his brother-in-law who lives next door?"

But his brother-in-law said, "You're never going to get this man. He hates the Church. He won't talk about it to anyone."

This man had come to Utah in the old CCC (Civilian Conservation Corps) program and stayed.

I told George, "We're going to baptize him. We've got to." I handed George the phone. "You call him."

He called and said, "Ernie, this is George Hatch. Remember me? I fish with you once in a while down at the harbor."

They talked a little, and then George continued: "I'm a stake missionary now for the Church, and I've been assigned to baptize you. I think I'd like to come over. I've got a man here with me, Herschel Pedersen, and we'll come over and see you right now."

"If you think you can baptize me, then you come over."

We walked around back, and there was Ernie standing in the gravel driveway with his wife, fire in his eyes. He was going to take on the Mormons right there.

George said, smiling, "Ernie, it's good to see you." He took hold of Ernie's hand and they started talking about catfishing. Then he introduced me.

We talked to Ernie there in the yard for about fifteen or twenty minutes. It was evident he didn't want to invite us in. Then his wife said, "Why don't we go in the house and sit down, where we can be more comfortable?"

We went in and talked for another twenty minutes or so, then asked if we could come back.

"Oh, yeah, you can come back anytime."

We baptized him three months later.

Before Christmas, we'd have the kids save up a little money, and our way of celebrating Christmas was for the whole family to take food baskets or an envelope with money to the families who were poor.

A story will show the effect of this practice on the kids. One summer when I worked at Geneva Steel, a freshman kid from Canada, a returned missionary who was married, worked for me. We became pretty good friends, and then he went back to school at BYU.

About Christmas time, I got a letter from him from Canada. He'd broken his back, his wife was pregnant, and he wrote that he'd worked at Geneva and had three days' back pay coming, but never picked up his check, because he didn't think he'd ever need the money. Now he had bills. Would I be willing to get the check and send it to him?

Sure enough, Geneva still had the check and gave it to me, about fifty dollars or so.

I came home and talked the situation over with the kids, asking them, "How would you feel if this was me?"

Every one of our kids not only wanted to send him his check, they also wanted to send some Christmas money. We had a meager Christmas, but I borrowed a little money from the credit union.

We had a wonderful Christmas morning, and in the afternoon, after the kids came back from seeing what all their friends got, and the friends came to see what my kids got, I reminded them that they had done something better than all that.

When this man recovered, we quit sending him the fifty dollars a month. He went on to get a PhD, and the last time I saw him, he was a stake president. He once asked me to come and speak to the young people in his stake. He later became a mission president.

What our family did for him also helped our children.

To show how children are, when I was a stake missionary, I'd been visiting a part-member family in the Ninth Ward. None of the children had been baptized, even though their mother was a member of the Church.

One night after I'd been teaching this family, I told my kids how the children in that family felt left out of the community. The kids had complained, "Just because we don't go to church, the other kids treat us rotten. We've lived here all our lives, but nobody befriends us, nobody talks to us." The mother complained about the same thing.

I phoned the bishop of that ward and asked if he'd talk to some of the parents and kids in his ward.

Then I asked my daughter Sheree, then in the ninth grade, "Do you know the daughter in this family?"

"Yeah, her locker's right next to mine."

"Then how about doing me a favor?"

"What's that?"

"I want you to go out of your way. You have a circle of friends here in the ward. I want you to befriend this girl."

"We'll try."

She talked to her friends, and they decided it would be a friendly gesture once in a while, so they started to befriend this girl.

About two weeks later I asked my daughter, "How are things going?"

"Dad, since we've befriended her, she just gloms onto us. We can't go anywhere, we can't do anything now, without her being there."

"That's all right," I assured her. "She's going to church, isn't she?"

"Well, yeah."

"Look, this girl has never had any friends who were active in the Church. She's always felt inferior. You'll find that she's as good as you are." I never knew that this type of discrimination existed in the Church.

Sheree continued to befriend the girl, and she has been one of her best friends, even to this day.

Chapter Twelve

Reactivation Work

I was asked to do some activation work in my stake. I was having conversations, mostly silent (I didn't want the devil to hear me), with the Lord: "I've fasted and prayed. I've read my scriptures. I'm trying to repent. I know that I've got a lot of faults, some I don't even know about. But we read in the Book of Hebrews 8:12, 'I will be merciful to their unrighteousness.'"

I continued, "I'm going to represent you, and I'm going to do the best I can. I'd appreciate it if you'd let the Holy Ghost be with me, because if it's not, nothing's going to happen. I can't do this on my own—if any good comes out of this, it has to be by the Holy Ghost."

I also went to the temple often, and if I was working with a particularly difficult situation—like someone I'd been visiting a dozen or more times—I'd put their name on the prayer roll. I'd fast and pray for maybe three days.

I know a lot of people think that's foolish, but then you look at yourself in the mirror and think, "You're supposed to visit this guy and get him to go to church, and he hasn't been active for thirty years." You know that his relatives have tried to get him to church, and his bishop has tried, and neighbors have tried. So I thought, "Who do you think you are that *you* can succeed? You know you've got to have a lot of divine help. You realize that after three days of fasting, the Lord may look down on you and say, 'I'm going to help this old boy this time.'"

I'd been a stake missionary for about five years when I was called to be a Mission Representative for the Quorum of the Twelve. But as soon as I was released, I was called to be a stake missionary again. Bill Green, the stake mission president, held a meeting each Tuesday night. (This was then part of the seventies' program, and I'd done the same thing when I was stake mission president.)

After the seven presidents met, the seventies in the stake and the stake missionary would join the meeting. We'd have a little prayer meeting, then go out and make visits, two by two. (If you let a man go alone and don't check up on him, he's inclined not to make his visits. That's also why I emphasized fasting and prayer.)

I was given an assignment: "Brother Pedersen, you're assigned with Doug Bennett." Doug has been home from his mission about a year and was now married. (Doug had been one of the missionaries present in Arizona when the Reverend Vincent McMurrow was converted in sixteen minutes.) We were handed a list of six names of nonmembers.

"That's all we get?" I asked.

"That's all you get."

There weren't a lot of nonmembers in American Fork at the time.

I pointed to a name on the list and announced, "We're going to baptize this man first." I'd visited him a long time before that and even thought he was ready for baptism.

The ward mission leader was not at all optimistic: "You'll never baptize him. That family is really hostile. The bishop can't get into the home. The Relief Society can't either. Not one person from the Church can get into that home?"

"What do you mean?" I protested. "The kids of the family were all in Boy Scouts, and they all went to church. It was just the parents who didn't go. And the man's wife is a cousin to one of the General Authorities."

"Nobody gets in!"

"I don't believe that."

So as soon as the meeting was over, I said to Doug, "Let's go visit this guy first. I know he's ready to be baptized."

Doug still wasn't very convinced. "Look, we've been there, and they wouldn't let us in."

"That's just the devil stirring something up. This guy is ready to be baptized."

"Are you sure?" Doug asked.

"Yeah, I just get feelings about these things."

"Okay," Doug allowed. "But you'll do the talking. I'm not going there and be told again where to go."

"That was last time. Let's go now."

One of my favorite passages that applies to this kind of situation is in D&C 100:5-8 (I've quoted it a thousand times): "For it shall be given you in the very hour, yea, in the very moment, what ye shall say." Then you're to bear your testimony.

"So Doug," I explained, "when we knock on the door and get in, and we've been talking for a few minutes, I want you to keep asking mentally, 'Lord, what do you want us to say to this man?' I'll do the same when you're talking. We'll have that kind of prayer in our minds and hearts while we're there."

When we knocked on the door the woman of the house answered. "Brother Pedersen, won't you come in? I haven't seen you for a long time."

Doug had a look of amazement on his face. But I'd been there many times before.

The husband was sitting there, attached to oxygen tanks, so I knew something was wrong—at one time he'd smoked two or three packs of cigarettes a day. I figured he had emphysema.

I called him by name and asked, "What in the world has happened to you?"

He started to tell me about his illness, and I was right—emphysema. I was praying silently, *Lord, what do you want me to say?* I glanced over to Doug, as if to ask, "Are you doing what I told you to?" The look on his face told me he was.

So I said to this man, "Tell me about your children."

"I'll let my wife tell you."

As she gave a little update of the children, I'm saying to myself, *Lord, when she finishes, what do you want me to say?*

I looked the couple over and then spoke, calling the husband by name: "I used to come here a lot of times. I taught you everything I knew about the gospel. Your kids all went to church. They're all gone now, and you're all alone. I'd like to ask you one question."

"What's that?"

"When are you going to be baptized?" The tears started running down his face, and Doug looked over at me.

The man answered, "Just as soon as you can help me quite smoking."

"That's wonderful. How many days do you need? Thirty?"

"I can't do it in thirty. I've been trying to stop for years. That's the only reason I'm not baptized. I've gotten bitter and everything else because I can't stop smoking."

"How about ninety days?"

"Okay, I'll try in ninety days."

"We'll come every week and give you a blessing. We'll work with you. We'll get some people to fast and pray for you. We'll get your active children to pray for you, because you'll need to have them sealed to you in the temple."

The wife agreed with all this.

I went on: "Who do you want to baptize you?"

"I want you to baptize me. You're the one who came all—"

"No, that would be wrong. Isn't brother So-and-so [the General Authority] your wife's cousin?"

"Yes."

"He's the one who ought to baptize you."

"But he looks down on us like we're trash. He won't even speak to us. We don't even go to family reunions because he acts so high and mighty."

"Is that the way *he* thinks or the way *you* think he thinks? Look, I know this man. He's a very humble man. In fact, he interviewed me when I married. He's a kind man, and I know he'd be glad to baptize you. I'm going to write him a letter, and if he says he's willing to baptize you, will you let him?"

"Yes, if he'll come down, I'd be honored."

"Good. Let's set your baptismal date." We pulled out a calendar and put down a Friday in February. I wrote the General Authority a letter, telling him that his wife's cousin's husband was going to be baptized, and we'd like to invite him down to baptize and confirm him, if he'd be willing.

The General Authority not only wrote *me* a letter, but also a letter to this man—a very compassionate letter, thanking him for the strides he was making and saying he would pray to help him give up his tobacco.

By Christmastime, this man was off tobacco and was coming to church, even though he could hardly walk. When the day came for his baptism, he was one of the sickest men I'd ever seen—flu, the sniffles. The day before the baptism, his wife called to beg off the baptism, because her husband was so sick.

I asked the man, "What do you want to do?"

"We're going to hold the baptism," he insisted.

So they came to the planned baptism, along with other family members, and we waited for the General Authority to arrive.

This man asked me to speak, and for about five minutes I talked about the meaning of the Holy Ghost and baptism—things I'd taught him many times. I bore my testimony, the General Authority arrived, and we went ahead with the baptism and confirmation.

That man never missed church until he died six months later. Of course he hadn't been in the Church long enough to go to the temple, but his wife had all that work done for him.

Yes, I can be overly aggressive at times. Sometimes a bishop would call me and say, "I don't want you to visit that family. You're too aggressive."

"You're right, but I'm going to anyway." I could be aggressive but not offensive. I've always thought of myself as kind of passive, and I always prayed for the families I visited. I've tried to be kind to them. When I challenged them, it was always like "You can do this."

We once visited a family that had to live in the filthiest house you could think of—dirty diapers in the corners, a terrible smell. The only room in the house that was at all clean was the front room, where we visited them. Everybody had visited them, but still they didn't come to church. The children were the same age as my children, and the wife was always pregnant and still had the last child in diapers.

The husband's attitude was the line that "everybody who goes to church is a hypocrite. Bishops do this, and bishops do that, and stake presidents do such and such."

I'd visited him for two or three years, and we'd become friendly. I helped him when he put in his sidewalk, and he came over when I put in my patio. I went fishing with him and his boys.

Still, every time I visited him, it was "You're all hypocrites."

I told him, "You know, you may be right. But you're the biggest hypocrite of all."

"I am?!"

"Yes, you tell us all how bad we are, and if you're not a hypocrite, you ought to have the courage to tell us that right from the pulpit."

"I'd love to do that," he answered.

"Good, I'll make arrangements with the bishop for you to speak in sacrament meeting."

"I'll do that."

I talked to the bishop, and even though he wasn't inclined to listen to me, he finally agreed to let this man speak. I returned to the fellow and explained, "You've got time in a sacrament meeting to make your comments."

The bishop was still skeptical. I didn't know what the bishop had planned for the rest of the meeting. "If this doesn't turn out well, you're going to have to be the other speaker."

I wasn't worried. I told the bishop, "When this brother gets up there, I don't think he'll have to guts to say what he says. I'm kind of calling his bluff."

The next time I went to see this fellow, he explained, "Look, I really don't want to do it right off. I ought to come to church a couple of times before I speak."

"How many times do you want to come?"

He came to church for two or three weeks, so we moved his hypocrite speech back. Finally he came, and his wife and kids were sitting there. He's sitting on the stand, and talk about nervous—he's really sweating. I'm down in the congregation praying for him.

Of course everybody in the ward knew this man, and they'd seen him coming to church those few weeks. They thought the bishop had just invited him to speak.

Herschel and Shirley's Mission Call, 1987.

He rose, took hold of the pulpit, looked around, and his face went bright red. "Brothers and sisters, I had some things I was going to say about members of the Church being hypocrites. But I've actually come to ask you to forgive me… Would you please forgive me? I've said all these bad things about a lot of you people, and honestly, most of them are wrong. I said them out of my pride because I wasn't conforming to the principles of the gospel. But I'm going to change. I want to take my family to the temple."

Then he sat down. The bishop called on me to be the speaker!

What a sight it was to see that man up there, after all those years. He went to the temple, his kids went to the temple, his boys went on missions.

The Good Book says to teach nothing but repentance.

When I'd go fishing with these men, or talk to them about football, after a few minutes I'd say a silent prayer: *Lord, we've talked for these few minutes, but I need to say something to this man. What do you want me to say?*

Then I'd say whatever came into my mind. I hadn't planned anything. I didn't worry whether what I'd say was good or bad. I didn't prepare a speech.

Well, I did plan a speech one time when I was a stake missionary. A nonmember, a former navy man, moved to the valley as a recruiter. The first place they lived was in American Fork, and they became angry because at first, the members were so friendly to them; then the members learned the family were nonmembers, and that they drank, and that the members wouldn't let their kids play with his kids. That really ticked the man off.

So they moved into another ward, the same ward I was in, in kind of a cul-de-sac. We visited them, and everything was going pretty good. We gave them a Book of Mormon.

I said to George, my missionary companion, "The next time we go there, we're going to commit this family to baptism." We had an appointment on a Thursday. "George, we've got to go to the temple on Thursday, and I'm going to prepare a lesson."

I spent about sixteen hours preparing what I thought was the best lesson I'd ever prepared in my life to persuade somebody to get baptized. At five o'clock that morning, I went to the temple and went through three sessions. Then I came home and went over everything I had prepared. I picked up my companion and we headed for the family's home.

We arrived at seven o'clock and had a prayer, but no preliminary talk. You see, I'm going to nail them. Well, after about ten minutes into that lesson, there was no more spirit there than you'd find in a bar downtown. I could see that the kids wanted to watch television, the wife was nervous, and I knew that the husband had his mind on the six-pack of beer in the fridge (he drank a six-pack about every night). He was waiting for us to leave so he could get started on it.

I felt terrible. I finally said to my companion, "I'm sorry. We came here today to invite this man to be baptized into the Church, but there's no spirit here. There's something wrong, and it's my fault."

I turned to the father: "Would you allow me to offer a prayer. We'll leave and come back another day."

He said that was perfectly all right. We knelt with the family and I offered a simple prayer. I was about as sad as I could be—knowing I had messed up so bad.

In my prayer, I said, "Lord, we came here tonight to visit this family, but we came unprepared. We did everything I thought we should do, even preparing a lesson, but I forgot to ask you what this family wanted to hear. So we're leaving.

"Would you overlook our faults and failings and permit the Holy Ghost to come and comfort this family and let them know that the Church is true in spite of us? I'm kind of asking you to take care of the trouble we've caused."

Then I told my companion that I was going home, feeling that I had so messed up that the Lord wouldn't help me if we visited another family that evening.

When I arrived home, my wife said, "You're home kind of early."

I told her what had happened—that I hadn't had a very good night.

When we visited people, I usually knew that the Holy Ghost was inspiring me, but this time, I hadn't been inspired, and that became a concern to me.

Before I left for work the next day, I got up early and read the scriptures for about an hour and a half. Then on the way to work I asked the Lord to forgive me, hoping that the next time I visited this family, things would go better.

Shortly after I came home from work that afternoon, my wife said, "Call Gloria. She wants you to call her immediately."

"But I was just there last evening."

"Well, she's called two or three times, and I've told her you would be home about this time.

So I called Gloria. "This is Brother Pedersen. What can I do for you?"

"Could you come over tonight?"

"I sure could."

"We're ready to be baptized."

"What?!"

I hung up the phone and called George, my companion. "The So-and-so family are ready to be baptized."

"What?!"

"Let's go."

George cancelled an appointment he had, and when we arrived, it was hard to believe what we found. The whole family were dressed in Sunday-go-to-meetin' clothes. The husband explained, "This is pretty humbling, but when you finished praying last night, my first thought was to go to the beer. My wife was going to turn the television on. But as I got up, a feeling came over me. I sat down and said to my wife, 'Please sit down for a minute.'"

She answered, "Yes, there was a special feeling here today."

He continued, "We just sat there as a family. I didn't get any beer. We didn't turn the television on. We just sat in absolute silence, probably for two hours.

"Finally I turned to my wife and said, 'This church has got to be true. We're going to be baptized.' I told my wife to call you the next day, and then we all went to bed."

That was quite an experience for the family—but for me too. My companion and I had gone unprepared, not realizing that there's more to teaching a person something than all the study you might put into a lesson. Had I taught that lesson, it probably would have been the worst lesson I ever taught in my life—because it wasn't what the Lord wanted the family to hear."

George baptized the family and I confirmed them.

The father was called back into the navy, stationed in San Diego. While he was there, his brother joined the Church, and his wife's relatives in the area started to join the Church.

Some years later when this brother retired from the navy, he came back to American Fork, but he hadn't been to the temple yet. The couple paid their tithing and within three months all went to the Provo Temple to be sealed.

Chapter Thirteen

Stake Missionary Preparation Class

When I taught the stake missionary preparation class at my home every Sunday evening, the requirement never changed: everybody had to read twenty-five pages in the Book of Mormon. It would take us about twenty-two or twenty-three weeks to finish it. When we finished, we just started reading it all over again. Sometimes we didn't meet on a Sunday, or if we had stake or general conference. Eventually forty-four of the fifty-five of these young men went on missions or were married in the temple.

It wasn't my personal interest in these young men that did it, it was the Lord's influence. I don't believe that any person begins life with faith in God. You have to have faith in some kind of person first. So just by my visiting with these kids consistently, they came to know I was always going to be there.

A young man in the Twelfth Ward never did go on a mission, but I went with him to the temple when he was married. Today he's a counselor in a bishopric. He'd been dating the girl he married, and I didn't hold it against him that he married instead of going on a mission.

The thing is, these kids believed in someone. Then they started reading the Book of Mormon. Helaman 15:7 says that reading the scriptures leads us to have faith in Christ. ("The prophecies of the holy scriptures...[lead]...them to faith on the Lord.") I think that's what my visiting did for them—I cared about them, they knew I'd be back, and I put a little pressure on them.

I'd say to them, "When you get shaped up and go on a mission, you'll thank God that you were able to change your life." I'd talk to them as though a mission was just going to happen—this from the first time I met with them. It wasn't "Do you want to go on a mission," it was "When you go on your mission." Then I'd try to get them to relate to the Book of Mormon.

After we read the first twenty-five pages, we'd give them the book. 1 Nephi 2:16 tells how Nephi believed all the words of his father. Compare that to Young Joseph Smith, a young kid, fourteen years old. His parents belonged to one church, other family members to another church. He had a problem: Which church should he join? So he went out and asked God which church was right.

Then I'd add,

"Now you've got a problem too. You belong to a church, and the Lord wants you to go on a mission. Your bishop wants you to go on a mission. Your parents want you to go on a mission. But maybe you don't want to go on a mission. So what should you do?

"Nephi had gone out and inquired of the Lord whether he should believe his father, and the Lord softened his heart and gave him an answer. He didn't rebel, like his brothers did. He was willing to follow his father. Maybe he felt that his father was just taking him on a camping trip, like the scouts go on. But he learned better.

"Tell the Lord, 'I don't want to go on a mission. What do *you* want me to do?' If you'll start praying about that, you'll probably have the first spiritual experience of your life. Even if the Lord wants you to go on a mission, you still have your agency. You don't have to go if you don't want to. But I can promise you, you will know if the Lord wants you to go or not. That will start to develop some faith in you."

As we were reading the Book of Mormon, I would bring in the Joseph Smith story. "Now Joseph Smith, when he was translating the

Book of Mormon, came to a verse on baptism. He went out and prayed, and what happened? John the Baptist came, and he and Oliver Cowdery went out and got themselves baptized and ordained to the priesthood. I want you to come to where you will desire to do what the Book of Mormon thinks is best for you. If you were a missionary, would you be willing to ask somebody to be baptized? Stop and think about that."

After a few weeks, we'd come to 2 Nephi 31, where seven times in fifteen verses Nephi invites the people to be baptized. I'd say, "Now look. You've been reading the Book of Mormon. You've read these verses. This is a big challenge—an invitation to be baptized. Can any of you remember ever reading these verses about baptism?" Most of the time nobody would raise a hand.

I'd continue: "The first time the Book of Mormon talks about baptism is in Lehi's vision. Lehi saw that John the Baptist baptized Jesus. Two chapters later, Nephi has the same vision. Then in 1 Nephi 20, there's another account of John the Baptist baptizing Jesus." I'd write these verses on the board.

"In 2 Nephi 9:23, Nephi commands every man, woman and child to be baptized. If you're a nonmember of the Church in the mission field and are being taught the gospel, you'll read three accounts of John baptizing Christ. You think, 'Well, I was baptized as a child.' As a missionary, you can then say, 'Well, the Lord commands you to be baptized.' In 2 Nephi 31, the Lord invites us seven times to be baptized." By that time, about a quarter of all people who read the Book of Mormon will consent to be baptized. In the fifteen years I was a stake missionary, that's how I approached people.

I'd also turn to Mosiah 18, which tells about the Waters of Mormon. "Alma asked the people, 'What have you against being baptized in the name of the Lord?'" (v. 10). The Book of Mormon is written to invite people to be baptized. This is the question to ask people who have read the Book of Mormon and felt the Spirit.

Then I'd move on to Alma 7, where Alma says, "Come and be baptized unto repentance, that ye may be washed from your sins, that ye may have faith on the Lamb of God...and witness it unto him this day by going into the waters of baptism (vv. 14-15).

"Whatever it is in your life, whatever your needs, the Book of Mormon will intensify them until they reach a high point. If you'll have an attitude that baptism is emphasized in the Book of Mormon, you will find your faith increase; and whatever you desire, the Lord will bless you with that.

I would spend a whole day teaching that doctrine and principle—talking about how the Book of Mormon applies to them.

Lehi, Nephi, and Joseph Smith prayed; Laman and Lemuel did not. These young inactive people in the stake could now go out themselves and experiment with prayer, and through that process gain a desire to serve a mission. So pretty soon, we were working ourselves out of a job with these inactive young people. One day the stake president called me to be a bishop, and the project was discontinued. Only five or six of these young people were left. It started in 1977 or 1978 and ended in 1984—six or seven years.

I learned a great lesson from a nonmember of the Church when I worked at Geneva Steel. I was at one time sent to a management "charm school," led by some guys from Harvard University. I called it all "blowing smoke," because there were so many smoke screens. These guys knew all the jokes and other ways to keep the people laughing, to keep the class moving. They were very motivational in that way.

Then one day the instructors started to talk about problems with discipline and the union, and they were getting down to the nitty-gritty of what management is like when you're on the front line, as we students were.

A fellow from Lorraine, Ohio, raised his hand and said, "If a man gets belligerent and rebellious and is mad, and you give him an either-or-else ultimatum, he'll take the 'or else' every time."

The instructors asked him, "Then what's the solution?"

"If you're a manager in a free country, working with people who have their agency, all you can do is motivate such a person. That person has to make the changes and do the work on his own. You can reprimand that person and send him home, but that just makes him more angry. You can compel him to work, but he'll hate you for it. You've got to be able to motivate people to *want* to work."

I'd faced this problem early on in my career at Geneva, and I found what this man said to be true. So when I taught these young people, if I could help them believe that what I was saying was true, or they believed that I really cared that they went on missions, that would motivate them. Through their reading, they felt the Spirit, and I suppose the Spirit helped me say some things now and then that helped them. In the end, I think it was the Lord blessing the young people because of their own efforts. Otherwise, I don't think a kid would put forth the same effort to go on a mission. Only the Lord can allow them to do it.

We had young women in the group too, though about forty were young men, and not a one of these young women ever went on a mission. They'd come to class, get jobs, clean themselves up pretty good, and then after two or three years of attending church meetings, they'd be off getting married in the temple.

I would tell them: "Don't ever tell the young man you marry about your past. If God has forgiven you, he's forgotten about it, and you should be able to forget about it too. Just be yourself, read the scriptures, and be the kind of mother your mother always wanted you to be. But don't tell other people about your past."

I told the young men the same thing: "When you go into the mission field, don't tell a single soul about your past. If you've repented, that's between you and your bishop." I would use D&C 108 as my theme. The first verse addresses Jared Cater, but what the Lord says to him he says to all: "Your sins are forgiven you, because you have obeyed my voice in coming up...to receive counsel of him whom I have appointed. Therefore, let your soul be at rest concerning your spiritual standing" (vv. 1-2).

When the bishop, the stake president, and the General Authorities clear a young man to go on a mission, then he has been declared worthy.

Verse three adds some counsel: "And arise up and be more careful henceforth in observing your vows, which you have made and do make." That's what I taught those young people—"Just don't mess up your life again, not the rest of your life."

If your sins have been forgiven, you shouldn't have guilt feelings when you are older and have a wife and kids. You don't revert and start thinking, "When I was a kid I messed up so bad." No, you've got to be faithful to your covenants, for the sake of your children, if nothing else. When I felt that a young man was ready to go on a mission, I'd call his bishop and say, "Bishop, this kid is coming to church. I'm visiting with him every week, and he seems to be coming along pretty good. What do you think?" Then I'd call the stake president and say, "I think this young man's about ready to go on a mission. How about interviewing him?"

I became a little wary, a little hesitant, of my approach when the bishops turned down the first two or three young men. I wasn't disappointed, but I did become more hesitant about recommending missions. I'm still a bit wary in calling young men, because I've known elders on missions who had done a lot worse things than some of the kids I was teaching had done.

One young man had been attending church only a year, and I thought he'd be turned down for sure and not be allowed to go on a mission. But this kid came to me with a big smile on his face. The stake president came out of his office, walked right over to the boy's parents, and said, "I want to tell you, you've got a wonderful boy here. He can go on a mission anytime you want to send him. I'll call the bishop and tell him."

This boy was the only young man who had been attending the class for only a year and been approved for a mission.

At one time, bishops gave quotas to ward members to go to the temple, based on the number of recommends or members in the ward. The last year I was elders quorum president, Bishop Gunther handed me 1,026 assignments for endowments.

I had one other assignment: I was put on a committee to plan ward conferences. The stake presidency approved that we ask the leaders of the ward to go to the temple one night, fasting and praying, in preparation for stake conference: the bishopric, elders quorum presidency, the Young Women and Young Men's leaders, and all other leaders. We'd have them go on a Wednesday night, and then on Thursday night a member of the stake presidency or high council would meet with them and talk about problems in the ward that should be addressed at stake conference.

When I was elders quorum president, each of the priesthood quorums and groups were given quotas for temple endowments to do, based on the number of temple recommends or people in the ward. The first year I was president, our quota was only two or three hundred. Later, we were given more than a thousand. I couldn't understand how the quota kept going up year after year.

I said to a counselor in the bishopric, "Look, summer's coming, and my elders don't want to go to the temple in June, July and August. School's out and the kids are home. It's been hard to get the people to go to the temple. Why don't we see if we can get our temple work quota met by June?"

"June?" he questioned.

"Yes, that shouldn't be too tough. We've got all fall, winter and spring to do the work."

I went to the quorum presidency meeting and announced, "We've got so many names for this year, and we'd like to do the endowments for them by June. Then we'll take the summer off. We won't have to ask the elders to go to the temple once during those summer months."

Elmo Murdock in the ward got up in elders quorum and said, "For every elder and his wife that go to the temple this Thursday, I'll take them to Harmon's Kentucky Fried Chicken afterwards and buy them a meal."

At one time, we had only eight elders in the quorum with temple recommends, though by this time we had many more.

When we called Harman's, they asked, "How many people will be here?"

Elmo answered, "Oh, reserve it for about sixty or seventy."

When we finally went, there were over a hundred people, and Elmo footed the bill.

After that, the elders quorum presidency selected eight elders each week. We gave each couple two couples to call and drive the group to the Salt Lake Temple. That was when the Salt Lake Temple was very crowded, and we sometimes had to wait forty-five minutes just to go through the veil.

We didn't mind the two-hour drive and the long sessions. We were getting the work done. A number of my quorum worked at Geneva, and they would have a certain number of days off each week. We'd go up for the first session at five o'clock in the morning.

We learned the traditions of the high priests at the Salt Lake Temple. When you went into the ordinance rooms at the temple, if you got on a certain row, you might be toward the front when you started, but when you came to go through the veil, you ended up in the last row. The high priests would say to us, "Oh, go on in. Go on in." But we found if we moved back, we'd end up on the front row. So we caught on to the tricks of the old high priests, and we'd respond, "Oh, no. You go ahead, Brother."

We'd go up and do five endowment sessions and a couple of ten-name initiatory sessions—working all day till the temple closed.

Come the first of April, we could see we'd get the thousand names done pretty easily, and by June, they were all done and then some more. At that time, the temple recorded your stake's name, so our stake got a report on how many names we'd done.

In August, in a priesthood executive meeting, my bishop said to me, "Brother Pedersen, you're the elders quorum president, aren't you?"

"Yes."

"We've got a little problem here. Not one of your elders attended the temple in either June or July."

"I know that, Bishop, and we're not going in August either."

"What?"

"We gave the elders the summer off."

"Why?"

"Have you looked at the report—the whole report? Our quota's done for the whole year. You gave us 1,026 names, and the elders have done them all. Come September, if you want, we'll help the seventies and high priests get theirs done. But that's only if you want us to." And come September, we finished up the seventies' and high priests' quotas.

The point is that people started going to the temple.

That fall in stake conference, a General Authority (Grant Bangerter) was our visitor. He'd been a regional representative when I was elders quorum president, and somehow he'd had a meeting with our stake president. He had interviewed my elders, so he knew how many of them had gone to the temple. He'd told Brother Bangerter about what had happened over a number of years. We'd activated four or five here, a few more there, maybe twelve a year. And these couples kept their recommends.

Later, when Brother Bangerter spoke in general conference, he said there was an elders president in American Fork by the name of Herschel Pedersen who had activated all members of his elders quorum except three.

That caused me more trouble than anything I'd ever said or done—I started getting phone calls from everywhere. Brother Bangerter asked me to go down and speak in St. George, and then he took me over to Page, Arizona. I didn't mind these opportunities—in fact, I enjoyed them. But as a result, I started getting even more calls and invitations to speak.

True, I still get invitations to speak in many places, to the point that it has at times been a burden. When I was called to be a bishop, at the time I was working with all the hippie kids, I was averaging six talks a week. I once spoke at five different sacrament meetings on one Sunday.

My talks were about whatever people wanted me to talk about. The men at Geneva who had become active in the Church were also being called to positions, and they were calling me to give talks.

The temple has always played a great role in everything I've done in my life. When I first started working with the inactive kids, or an inactive family, I would go to the temple at least once a week for a period of six to eight weeks, even before I visited a family. I'd keep the family's names on the prayer roll. In Alma 16:16, we read, "The Lord did pour out his Spirit on all the face of the land to prepare the minds of the children of men, or to prepare their hearts to receive the word which should be taught among them at the time of his coming."

The Holy Ghost has a responsibility: it is supposed to go over the land to prepare the hearts of the people, but I'm the one who's supposed to go do the teaching. That's why I would fast, pray, and read the scriptures, then try to keep an open mind when I visited a family. Then as I went to the temple, I'd count the weeks: "In six weeks, I'll be visiting the family. In five weeks, I'll be going," and so on.

CHAPTER FOURTEEN

FAMILY CHALLENGES

One challenge in our marriage was my shift work at Geneva. If I was at work all day and then had to work graveyard, it was difficult trying to sleep when we had as high as three kids in diapers at the same time. Also, I just wasn't around at times when Shirley needed me when we were raising the children, though that turned out to be an advantage after the kids got older. In the summertime when I worked afternoon shift, I could get up early in the morning and garden or do things with the kids before I had to go to shift work.

The bad part of shift work was that at times I couldn't get to my Sunday meetings. For a number of years, I had only four Sundays off every three months, though I'd never miss my meetings except when I had to work the day shift. Of course if I had a bad night on the midnight shift, I'd be tired.

Yet shift work and having days off in the middle of the week were also an advantage, especially in the summertime, so I was able to do many things that others could not do. Where other fathers had to work, I could take my children on an outing or picnic. I'd come home about eight in the morning, eat some breakfast, then sleep till about one or one-thirty in the afternoon. Then I'd go out and visit the inactive elders until about seven or eight o'clock in the evening. After that, I'd eat and get another hour's sleep before I went back to work.

I was also able to do my missionary work, even though I had a large family. Time especially became a priority when I was called to do a lot of stake missionary work and visit inactive elders. When we re-activated some of the elders, we'd invite three or four of the families to family home evening at our home on Monday nights. Shirley would bake some pizza and we'd have root beer. I taught the lessons. Every week, it was two or three different families.

We also always raised a garden. Max Bond lived about a quarter of a mile from me, and he had ten acres of land. We were friends, and in fact we worked together. One day I said to Max, "You've got all that land, and all you do is raise hay. Why don't we put an acre and a half or two acres into a garden?"

"I'll tell you what," he said. "I've got the land and the water, and a tractor. You come over and plow what you want as a garden, and as long as you plant it and take care of it, we'll kind of share it. You have your kids come over and weed, and I'll help a little with the weeding" (though that never happened).

A kind of ditch ran through the middle of the acreage. I made a suggestion: "Why don't we get rid of that ditch there and take it over here?"

On my days off, I'd kick the kids out of bed at five in the morning, and we'd work in the garden for two or three hours and then take care of the yard. The kids didn't like getting up that early, but they knew that the work was scheduled at that time.

So for many years, our family had a huge garden, probably an acre and a half. One year we had two hundred tomato plants, and we used to raise so much corn we couldn't give it away. On my days off, my kids and I would go over and weed the garden. I'd tell the kids, "You can't go out with your friends, you can't do anything until we go weed the garden." We'd take our hoes and do that one day every week until later in the fall. Once the plants grew and spread out, there weren't so many weeds. But then we'd have to put the corn up.

When we gardened, sometimes a child would chop out a corn plant. I'd say to the kid, "What's the matter with you? We plant corn to raise corn, and now you've chopped a plant out." This would usually happen when they were in a hurry to go someplace. One day I said to my son, "When you get those ten rows hoed, you can go."

He came and said he'd done all them. "I'll tell you what, son. I'll bet I can find ten weeds you've missed in twenty-five yards." I found that many. Then I said, "I'll tell you what. I'll bet you can find a hundred weeds in my row too." This was to show that none of us is perfect in weeding.

I used to go fishing a lot, one of my ways of helping get inactive men to go to church. As the kids came along and grew older, I could see that I would have some kind of problem if I didn't spend more time with them. So I started taking my kids fishing, Wayne to the Provo River when he was just five or six years old. One day in a heavy runoff year, Wayne almost drowned, so that was the end of my fishing in the Provo River, though he caught a four-pound trout that day, and I caught six smaller ones. His fish was bigger than all mine put together.

During the summers, at least every other week, sometimes weekly, if I had a day off in the middle of the week, the kids and I would get up at four o'clock and go fishing someplace. Sometimes we'd fish from the shore, but later we rented a boat for a day out of Clark's Camp for two or three bucks. It always seemed the Lord blessed us so that we were the luckiest fishermen on the face of the earth. I'd fished there many times with a lot of the old timers, so I knew from them where there were some deep holes out on the reservoir. We didn't have a motor on the boat, so we'd just keep rowing till we found one of those holes. There we'd put our anchor down and fish.

We'd have kind of a contest, and we always got our limit in two or three hours. Next we'd have a picnic and finally bring home a whole bunch of fish.

Shirley would put together a picnic of sandwiches, cookies, candy and soda pop, or whatever we wanted to eat, and sometimes she would go with us.

A friend of mine, who we called "Old Killer Gordon," had a pontoon boat, and also a cabin at Strawberry. He'd say, "Here, take the boat and your big bunch of kids. Here's the keys." That made for an especially great day of fishing and joking and telling stories. If Shirley didn't come with us, we'd come home in the afternoon, and she would have dinner waiting for me. I'd be out visiting my inactive boys by eight o'clock, come home, eat something, jump out of my suit and into my work clothes, and go to work. If I was working graveyard, I'd do my visiting in the afternoon. On the day shift, I could be home by five, eat, and be out visiting till nine or so in the evening.

It was out in the garden and on the boat where I taught the kids the gospel. On the boat, I'd tell them all kinds of stories, and we'd talk about the gospel and about things that happen in the world. Because it was kind a playful family situation, they got so they'd ask questions. I would tell them Bible stories—like the story of Elijah calling down fire from heaven to set fire to the altar, which the false priests couldn't do. Out on the water, I could dramatize it, because there'd be nobody around. The kids would ask questions.

Then a real problem did come up. I didn't realize how many hours I was putting in. When I was elders quorum president, I visited every elder once every three months. One night, just a few months before I was released as quorum president, Jimmy Cates, my first counselor, was supposed to pick me up. He arrived as I was putting my shoes on. Shirley turned to him and asked, "Jimmy, why don't you do me a favor? Tell the elders president to visit his wife and family once in a while." As I went out the door, I said, "Okay." I got to thinking to myself, *What are you doing? While you're out visiting all these people, are you neglecting your family?*

That's when I started staying home more, realizing it was tough leaving Shirley home with the kids all the time. I started doing things with the kids in the evenings. I still visited my elders, just not as often.

This is also when I started to buy season tickets to the BYU football and basketball games. Shirley liked to go to the games as much as I did. We also took some of our kids with us.

One cold night when we had Gary Nelson, the little Indian boy in our home; BYU was playing Arizona State in football. Because it was cold, the kids wanted to go to a movie instead, so I asked Gary, "Do you want to go to the game or to the movie?" He said yes, which in Navajo culture meant he wanted to do both, so he didn't realize he was supposed to be making a choice. So I asked him, "If you could only do one, which would you rather do?" He said, "I want to go to the ballgame with you." As I recall, some of the other kids also came, and we also took a neighbor boy. Some went with Shirley to the movie. The little girls who went with me put on their "88" sweatshirts, in honor of Phil Odle, a BYU football star at the time.

We did a lot of fun things like that as a family.

My time away from my family eventually came to a head in another way, so we had a family home evening, what I called "Rip-Dad Night." I said to Sheree, who seemed to be the most critical, but probably also the most compassionate of my daughters, "You're going to be the scorekeeper." (Sheree cares deeply for people. She worries about people, just like I worry about people. I believe she inherited the trait from me, so she may be the second best worrier in the family.)

Then I said to my littlest one, Sherlyn, "This is Rip-Dad Night. You can say anything you want about your father—what I do wrong, what I need to do better, what I need to do more of."

"Well, Dad, you don't play with me enough."

I said, "Good. Write that down, Sheree."

We went through the whole family, right up to my wife. It's not the most pleasant thing to do in life—not the first time, anyway, especially if you've got nine kids, and some of them are teenagers. As each one of those children spoke up, I had quite a list of things to work on.

I may not have agreed with some of the things they said—they were a little out of place in the family—but that was only my thinking. In their minds, that's the way things were, so I accepted them. "Okay," I said, "I accept this, and I'm going to work on it." Sheree added each complaint to the list.

A month later, I was doing the best I could. I may have shortened up in some areas, but in general, I was doing a lot better. For one thing, I quit reading the scriptures as much—I'd considered it a must to read all the standard works four times a year. Cutting back on my reading gave me some time to do things with the kids.

The next month, when we had another Rip-Dad Night, I got the report. We went down the list, and each of the kids said I'd improved some on their complaint.

I made this process a regular thing over the next few years.

It got pretty soon that there weren't many things on the complaint list, so it was something I needed as a father. The kids were leaving home for school, missions and marriage. Had we not had those Rip-Dad Nights, I'd probably have become the most fanatical person on the face of this earth, doing nothing but reading the scriptures and visiting people. The Lord was now blessing my good children. They were still always going to church, but we had started to do things as a family.

My children and grandchildren now come to our home almost once a month for a study session. They come with their scriptures and their notes, and we talk about anything they want to talk about. I didn't force this on them; they asked for it. They write up what we discuss and send it to the family members who aren't present.

A recent lesson had to do with the scattering of Israel. We went through what the Book of Mormon has to say on the gathering of Israel and what we are to expect in these latter days. I'd cut from the newspapers reports of events happening in Israel and Palestine, and in the islands of the sea. We read in 1 Nephi 20, where Nephi says the Lord remembers the isles of the sea, how the Lord had hidden people in the isles of the sea, but in the right time, they'll be identified and set free. "The Book of Mormon talks about *your* day," I told my family.

We talked about temple building, how temple work will set free the prisoners who are in the spirit prison. "Look at the building of the temples. Look at how it relates to your life. If you'll read your patriarchal blessing, you'll see that you have a part to play in this great work. These temples are being built for *you*."

When these kids leave, they ask, "Grandpa, when are we going to have another study group?"

I answer, "When do you want one?"

We schedule another one, they all come, and I ask, "What do you want to talk about?"

We start talking, and the blessings of the Lord pretty soon start pouring out of me. My children will all agree that somehow the Lord has blessed me to be able to remember where the right scriptures are when we start talking about something. I don't have to look them up; they just kind of pop up in my mind.

The other day, I told my grandson, "Read 2 Nephi 22:8."

"There's not that many verses in chapter 22," he explained.

"I told you wrong. I mean 1 Nephi 22:8." Once in a while, I'll make a mistake.

DATING AND DRIVING

I was a pretty good-natured dad most of the time, though I was rather stern with the children. They always had good friends, people who are now bishops and doctors and so on. We never had a bad kid come in to our home. But as the family grew older, we developed a problem. When the kids were in high school, they wanted to go here, they wanted to go there, with those friends. As an old conservative man, raised kind of in the depression, I hadn't done all those things. When they'd ask, "Dad, can I go here…or there?" I'd say, "Well, I don't know. Who's going?"

They'd answer, "Everybody's going—everybody."

"Who's *everybody*? I'm not going, and I'm somebody."

"You know, all my friends."

"Who of your friends are going?" Then the kids would start naming them, and we knew them all. Most of them lived in the ward.

Then I'd ask, "Is this a wholesome type of thing you're going to be doing?"

"Oh, yes, it is."

Sometimes I'd say they couldn't go, and sometimes Shirley and I would talk about it. I just didn't know what was right in some of these things, such as a movie they'd be going to. So I'd ask, "What's the name of the movie?"

We had a problem: What's a good movie and what's a bad movie? What's good music, and what's bad music?

Whether I said yes or no got to be kind of a problem. Social values were changing at the time.

One day when Sheryl was in high school, she wanted to go somewhere with her friends and drive my old Dodge truck, whose floorboards were out and everything else run down. My thought was that the safest thing to say was absolutely no. Instead I said to her, "You always say there's a credibility gap between parents and kids, a generation gap. I'll admit I'm an old fogey, and I don't understand all this modern stuff. I'm content to go to work, go to church, garden, and do a little hunting and fishing. I don't have much aspiration to do much more than that. I just want to see my kids raised in righteousness.

Herschel and Shirley's nine children who, as Herschel says, are "all sons, but eight!"

"You've asked me a question, and I don't know whether I should say yes or no. I don't know if what you want to do is right or wrong, but God does. You go to your room and have a little prayer, to see if God wants you to do it or not."

That became kind of the rule we followed in our house. Sometimes it worked, but once in a while it didn't. Three serious problems came up as a result of that policy.

Shauna was dating a guy, and we disapproved of him. It wasn't that he was bad, he just wasn't going to go on a mission. So we tried to discourage him from dating Shauna. Shirley and I fasted and prayed about it.

Every time we said something negative about the boy, Shauna would cry and defend him, and that made it all worse. Then one day I said to Shirley, "I'll tell you what. Let's have Shauna invite him over to dinner. Let's start treating this guy right and try to change our attitude, to make Shauna think we're not opposed to him."

He came over to dinner on Sunday, and he turned out to be a polite and otherwise well behaved young man. We started treating him well.

One day I said to Shauna: "You've reached the age where you really ought to have your patriarchal blessing." It was the fall of her senior year, and she was excited about being a senior.

"Yeah," she said. "I've been thinking about it."

"Why don't we fast every Sunday for the next three weeks? Then we'll get your patriarchal blessing and see what the Lord has to say to you."

So we fasted and talked about patriarchal blessings. All the kids listened to our discussions. We also fasted the day Shauna was to get her blessing, but I'd also been fasting a few days between Sundays, thinking we needed some inspiration, because now we're treating this kid with respect, but we still don't want Shauna to marry him. *We've got to break this up somehow.*

The patriarch gave Shauna a wonderful blessing. We all sat there crying. When we came home, while sitting at the table, I reminded her about how wonderful the blessing was. Then I asked Shauna if Shirley and I could go down to her room with her and talk about some of the things we had heard in the blessing. This was while Shauna was still crying with happiness.

A couple of days later, while I was reading my scriptures at the table (we read the scriptures for half an hour or forty-five minutes every morning as a family) the phone rang, Shirley answered it, and it was for Shauna. She handed the phone to Shauna, who nodded that it was the boyfriend, though I already knew it.

She said to him, "Look, I got my patriarchal blessing a few days ago, and I've been thinking about it. I've decided I'm going to marry a returned missionary. If you don't want to go on a mission, don't call me anymore."

That's how the problem was solved. Other problems that were just as critical also got solved by fasting and praying and having the kids be responsible to the Lord. We still had the little bumps and bruises, and each of the children was somewhat different.

There's a little conspiracy that goes on in every family, sometimes with the children, sometimes with the wife. Especially if I wasn't home, it was sometimes "Don't tell Dad"—because I was the sort of strict one.

Sharlene was always outgoing. She was now a senior in high school but she didn't have her driver's license yet. Once in a while, Shirley would let her take the car, especially if she'd be home before Dad got home.

On a particular Friday night in the spring of the year, when I came home from work, the car was parked in the breezeway. When I got up the next morning—Saturday was my day off—nobody said a thing to me as I got ready to do some work in the garden. They were still in bed anyway, from having stayed up late to watch TV or something.

When I went to the garage to get a tool or something, I looked at the corner of the car, and I knew there'd been a wreck. There was black and white hair, and blood, down the side of the car, and the door wouldn't open. I didn't get upset. I just went to work in my garden and started to think about what I should do.

When I returned to the house, I said to Shirley, "The car got wrecked last night."

"Yes," she explained, "I bumped into another car downtown."

"You did?"

"It's really not serious, just a little bump on the front."

"Maybe so, but one headlight's out."

"I meant to tell you when you came home."

"But you *didn't* tell me." By then, some of the kids were up, and they weren't saying anything either.

"A cow hit the car," I said. "How did a cow get downtown? There's blood all over the front of the car, and black and white hair. It had to be a Holstein cow you hit."

Shirley's face went red. I still wasn't angry.

She came out and took a look at the car, and her face went red as a beet.

"Let's go back in the house," I suggested, "and when you get time, I'd really like to know what happened." I went back to work in the garden.

By now, Shirley had Sharlene and all the kids were up. Sheree, who was still little, said, "Boy, you really messed it up now. We won't have any Christmas because we've got to fix the car, and it takes money to fix a car."

Here came Shirley and Sharlene, and Sharlene is just a bawlin'. "Dad, I'm sorry."

I said to her, "It's really not your fault. Your mom let you take the car, and you don't have a driver's license." Then Sharlene explained how the accident happened. She had hit a cow up in Alpine.

Then I looked at my wife: "Why have you supported Sharlene in a lie?"

"I knew you'd be mad at Sharlene, because you don't let the kids drive without a license." She reminded me that the car was already ten years old, and we usually bought a new car every ten years.

The family all talked about it, and we had a bad Saturday. I just worked in my garden.

About two o'clock in the afternoon, I came in the house. Shirley said, "You know something? I think we ought to buy a new car."

The next Saturday, I took all the kids and we bought a new car. You see, these little family conspiracies don't work.

Another time, Shirley phoned me at work to say that Sharlene was stuck in a snow bank up in Alpine.

I was just getting off work, so I came home and we went up to Alpine with my old 4-wheel drive Ford truck. There was Sharlene. A bunch of people were trying to help her get her car out of the ditch by putting rocks under the wheels, spinning the wheels, and so forth. They didn't have another 4-wheel drive truck, and they didn't have a chain. In the wintertime, I always threw a big tow chain in my truck, so I just hooked on to the car and pulled it out.

Sharlene was bawlin', but at least she did have her driver's license this time.

That was one of our few minor problems.

Chapter Fifteen

Mission Representative

After being at Geneva several years, in 1972 I began to go to the Salt Lake Temple and spend the entire day there, from when it opened till when it closed. Friends, either from the plant or the ward, would go with me. So we'd do something like twenty to twenty-five endowments a month during the winter months. I was elders quorum president, but only about eight of us elders had temple recommends, and we were trying to activate the others, four or five at a time (all eventually became active except three). It was kind of a process. One guy would say to another, "Well, I ought to go to the temple someday." He'd start thinking about it, tell his wife what he was thinking, and pretty soon they'd be at the temple. With me, it wasn't a rush-rush thing. I was planning on it being a career, thinking that our goal would be an eighth of an inch per week. If it took us twenty years to get everybody to the temple, that would be good enough.

In fact, I worked with one guy for twenty years before he finally quit smoking and three years later went to the temple. I once asked him, "How does it feel not that you've quit smoking for three years?"

He replied, "I never did quite smoking."

"But I've never seen you with a cigarette."

"That's right. I haven't smoked in three years, but that doesn't mean I've quit. Every time I see somebody light up a cigarette, the craving comes back. I just have to compel myself not to smoke."

His boy went on a mission the same day my son did.

In February 1972, a cold wintery day, I had gone to the Salt Lake Genealogy Library, when it was housed in the old Montgomery Ward building. I'd been going there every Wednesday since October and spent the entire day there. But I never found a name, and I was becoming very discouraged. When I'd gone up that cold and frosty day, about five o'clock in the morning, it was a beautifully clear morning. Now, at five o'clock in the afternoon, there was a blizzard. As I was coming down past the Point of the Mountain in my old, red Ford truck (two-wheel drive) at about ten miles per hour, all I could do was follow somebody's tail lights in front of me.

All of a sudden, his brake lights went on. I put on my brakes, and pretty soon there was a series of big collisions—boom, boom, boom! Everybody piling into each other. My truck wouldn't run—the radiator was broken. I hadn't taken an overcoat with me that morning. No highway patrol was present, and no ambulances. I wasn't hurt, but my truck had spun around into the middle of the street. I knew I'd better get out of my truck, in case somebody came along and hit me.

Sure enough, I had no sooner got out into the median than another car came, and wham! he hit my truck and spun it around. By now, I was sitting in the truck of the guy behind me, whose motor and heater were still running, even though the truck was all banged up.

When it started to clear, we could see that forty-six vehicles had piled up, including the bus that had spun out and caused the wreck.

I decided at that time that going to the library wasn't worth it. I made an agreement with my brothers that they would do the research and my family and I would do the ordinances.

That night, the thought came to me, *You are going to be called to a position in the Church that doesn't even exist.* I thought about that for a while, then concluded, *Maybe I'm really on the road to apostasy now.*

This has got to be foolish. I would go back to the temple and try not to think about it. But then while I was driving to work, the thought would come back. It got to where it began to bother me.

One hot day in May, my neighbor, who was tending my children so I could get some sleep, called to me, "You're wanted on the telephone."

I told her, "My wife tells them that I'll call them back."

"Oh, this is Elder Romney," she explained.

"Nancy, don't pull jokes on me." (She was kind of a joker anyway.) "I'm on graveyard shift, and I'm not in the mood for anything humorous."

"It's the truth. It's Elder Romney of the Quorum of the Twelve."

"I don't believe that. No one from the Quorum of the Twelve would ever call me for anything. If they do, it's because I'm in bad trouble."

I picked up the phone and said, "Hello."

The voice said, "This is Elder Romney of the Quorum of the Twelve. Do you know who I am?"

"I sure do, Elder Romney."

"How's your health?"

"Pretty good."

"How's your wife? And your kids? How many do you have?"

"I've got nine."

"Well, I've been told to call you."

"Yes, sir. What can I do for you?"

"We'd like you to be a mission representative to the Quorum of the Twelve."

"What's that? I don't know what that is?"

"It's a new position we're creating. It won't involve too much time, just a trip once in a while on weekends to visit a couple of missions for us. It'll be easy. Nothin' to it. All you've got to do is say yes."

So I said, "Yes, I'll do it."

"It's good you said yes. I'll tell the Quorum. Somebody will be in contact with you to tell you what you have to do."

When my wife came home, I told her what had happened. She asked, "What's a 'mission representative to the Quorum of the Twelve?'"

"I don't know. I only know that Elder Romney called."

A few days later, a letter came in the mail that explained some of things my wife and I were to do. First, we were to attend a seminar in the old Edison School across from the Church Office Building June 26 through 28.

I looked at my schedule: *I am in trouble. I've got to work those days. How can I be up there?*

Once in a while you could trade a day's work with someone else. I started to think, *I'll call George, the general foreman. He hates the Church, so he won't want to change my schedule if I tell him I'm going to a Church meeting.*

I prayed about it. It was easy to trade a day if I wanted to go pheasant or deer hunting, but I'd never asked anyone to trade anything for the Church. I was reluctant to do that.

It so happened that I was supposed to go to work that Monday, and in the afternoon, I was to spell the general foreman. I was called to the office and asked if I would be willing to do some double time. Someone was sick that week and wanted to use his vacation time. If I worked doubles for the next two or three days, I could have Thursday, Friday and Saturday off.

So I didn't have to work out a trade, though I did have to work sixteen hours a day.

I went to Salt Lake City, and as I walked to the door of the meeting room, there stood Elder Romney. "I'm Brother Romney," he said.

"I'm Brother Pedersen."

"I don't know you, do I?" he asked.

"No, I don't think you do, but you are the one who called me on the phone."

"Oh, then you were called properly, weren't you?"

I sat clear in the back, because I didn't know anybody there. Then Orville Gunther came in, and Grant Bangerter, and Stuart Durrant.

Elder Ezra Taft Benson, the president of the Quorum of the Twelve, conducted the meeting. (President Kimball had had open-heart surgery at the time, so he was not present.) All the new regional representatives were there too.

President Benson began: "Twenty-nine of you have been called to be mission representatives of the Quorum of the Twelve." Then he explained that we would be visiting the missions of the Church.

We would each be assigned a certain number of missions and would be expected to visit each mission for a week at a time. We would attend mission president seminars around the world.

I said to myself, *There is no way this is going to happen.*

I rode home with Orville Gunther in his fancy car, but I didn't say anything. Finally I said, "They've got the wrong guy. If God ever made a mistake calling somebody, this is it. I've never been anything but an elders quorum president and stake missionary, though I've done a little work with in the Senior Aaronic committee, visiting inactive people.

When I voiced my reservations to my wife, she said, "The Lord has called you."

When I returned the next day, I was very tired, and I was thinking about resigning from the calling. I listened to the instructions, took notes, came home and slept maybe three or four hours. I got up early and began to prepare my resignation speech. I hadn't been set apart yet.

That morning, I was very nervous! I didn't know who to tell that I wanted to resign. No General Authorities were present except President Benson, who, after the opening prayer, stood up and said, "Will Herschel Pedersen and So-and-so go over to Harold B. Lee's office. You are the only two who haven't been set apart. He's been out of town for a week, so he will now set you apart."

So there I was, in President Lee's office, somewhat embarrassed. (I've always felt inferior when I'm around General Authorities—out of place, very uneasy, a misfit, or something like that.) President Lee read my mind: "I know exactly how you feel, but don't say anything. Just sit down here, and I'm going to talk to you for a minute."

"Yes, sir."

He continued: "I knew your father and mother. I was your stake president. I spoke at your mother's funeral. Your father and mother were some of the greatest people ever in this Church. Your mother was a gifted teacher, and the same gift will be passed on to you. You will be a great teacher. We have had nothing to do with calling you to this position. The Lord has called you. He knows your problems. I'm now going to set you apart. When I'm finished, if there is anything you want to say, you can say it."

He probably knew my feelings.

He told me not to write down what he said to me, just to remember it. He said the Lord was pleased with the progress I had made in life. Wherever I went, at least two angels would be assigned to go with me so I wouldn't make any bad mistakes. The Lord would inspire me in the decisions I made. The Lord would bless my wife and children, and he would bless my work.

(As I later thought about the blessing of angels assigned to me, I realized that every time I boarded an airplane to carry out this calling, it seemed like angels were with me.)

After the blessing, he said, "I understand that you work at Geneva Steel."

I said, "Yes, and I am going to have trouble getting off work as many times as Brother Benson said we would have to go."

He instructed me, "I want you to meet with your supervisors and tell them that if they will cooperate with you and let you do this work for the Church, the Lord will bless each one of them personally. He will bless the plant, and he will bless their families. That is what I want you to go tell them. And tell them that a prophet said that."

"I'd be glad to do that," I said.

So I didn't resign but returned to the meeting. Half the General Authorities were now present, and there were only twenty-nine of us mission representatives. It was to be a testimony meeting.

I leaned over to Orville Gunther and said, "Orville, I don't know what I'm going to do, but I am *not* going to stand up. I'm *not* going to bear my testimony in the presence of these brethren. I am *not* worthy to be here……"

If there had been a crack in the floor, I'd have gotten through it. I was terrified!

S. Dilworth Young, who was conducting the meeting, said, "Brethren, four hours are allotted to this testimony meeting, more than enough time for all of you to bear your testimonies."

My heart started to pound. I thought about walking to the bathroom and just keeping right on going. But I couldn't do that. That would be a disgrace.

President Romney was asked to bear his testimony first. He said, "Brethren, a testimony is a very sacred thing. It must be borne in solemnity, and it must be borne with the proper thoughts. My testimony is very simple. I know God and He knows me."

Then he sat down.

President Joseph Fielding Smith then spoke for four or five minutes and bore a similar testimony, though in different words. I looked at my watch: *Four hours?!*

Each of the Brethren stood and bore the same testimony as Brother Romney.

Brother Hinckley gave us some instructions on dressing very conservatively.

Then everybody in the room had borne their testimony except the twenty-nine of us and Brother S. Dilworth Young. He stood and bore his testimony: "I'm going to bear the same testimony as Brother Romney and the others. In the name of Jesus Christ, Amen."

That's all he said, except, "Brethren, because none of you has a testimony like these, I want you to go back across the road and listen to the testimonies of your brethren."

My thought was, *I have escaped!*

One wealthy brother bore his testimony, thanking God that he had been blessed with money, a car, and this and that, so he could donate to the Church. Brother Young, now sitting next to me, asked me, "How does that compare with you have heard?"

"It doesn't compare."

"Why don't you go home, then?"

At seven that same evening, Elder Thomas Monson of the Quorum of the Twelve called me: "Brother Pedersen, you were set apart today as a mission representative. You've been assigned to the California East, California South, the California, and the Arizona Missions.

Herschel carrying the torch for the 2002 Winter Olympics in Salt Lake City, Utah.

"I also want you to know that President Joseph Fielding Smith passed away half an hour ago. Harold B. Lee will be the next president of the Church."

My calling had been announced in the *Church News*, so everybody at Geneva knew that I was now a mission representative for the Twelve. I was being congratulated. Then I asked if I could meet with my supervisors. The Lutheran, the Catholic and the apostate Mormon asked me to come at three in the afternoon.

"What do you want? Are you going to quit?" they asked me.

"No, I haven't come to quit. I have a message for you from the prophet." That's just how I said it.

They looked at me, and I saw something in their eyes. They hadn't been bothering me after all these years, because of my reputation for hard work, and they knew that members of the Church respected me.

I continued: "The message from the prophet is this: If you will cooperate with me and let me have a little time off once in a while, so I can do this work for my church, the Lord will bless each one of you personally. He will bless each and every member of your family. He will bless the entire plant. That's the word of the prophet. I've now said what the prophet asked me to say, so what do you have to say?"

The head person, the Lutheran, looked at me and said, "Look, what you do on your days off is none of my business." The Catholic said the same thing. Then they added, "You owe us forty hours a week, and we'll get them."

"Yes, sir," I said.

I had one week of vacation coming, and the first week of September, I was supposed to go to the Arizona Mission for a whole week. In October, I was scheduled to go the California South Mission. There were two other missions, plus a whole week of mission presidents seminars in San Francisco. It's now July. I have eight weeks of frustration and worry.

I started fasting two or three days a week and going to the temple. *Lord, I don't know how I'm going to do this. The plant is going to get its forty hours a week. But there's no way I can do this. I should have resigned the calling—but President Lee set me apart, and he's the prophet. You know my problems. What am I going to do?*

I was in a state of turmoil. I'd been released from all other callings (I was the stake mission president at the time, as well as the senior president of the stake seventies).

Along about the first week of August, a number of us were summoned to a big meeting in the church building across from the Geneva plant (Geneva had bought the Vineyard chapel to use for meetings for management). I went, expecting the worst.

Jednoff, the superintendent, stood up and said, "Gentlemen, in the past, whenever there has been an emergency or breakdown, you men have had to work overtime, but you've never been paid for it."

My first thought was that the plant would start paying us for the overtime.

"Well, I've got news for you. You'll not be paid for overtime, but the company has made a new policy. As of the first of August, all management will be given a compensatory hour for every hour you work overtime. How many days you can have off will be at the discretion of your supervisor."

This was good news to me. If I worked enough overtime, often enough, that would mean I could have three to four days off from time to time. All I had to do was find ways to get overtime.

When there were breakdowns, I was usually asked to stay and work. If people were sick, they often asked me to work their shift. In the winter, I've often had to work sixteen hours a day for as long as ten days.

This meeting was on Monday. On Tuesday, I was on swing shift as spell foreman, working as an "A" blower on vacations. My Catholic superintendent asked me to come to his office when I arrived at work.

"Am I in trouble?" I asked him.

"No, but I want to talk to you."

I knew it had something to do with work.

"We appreciate the way you've always been willing to work overtime and to cooperate. It doesn't matter what we've asked you to do, you've always been congenial. We have a major problem right now that I'd like to talk to you about."

"What's that?"

"Orson Hancock, from Payson, has had a severe heart attack, and we're in the middle of a vacation season. You're spelling as a blower, you're working on the furnaces, and you're spelling as a general foreman. We simply don't have any qualified hourly men to move up on the job of substitute foreman. I'm wondering if you'd be willing to work that for a while."

"How long do you want me to work?"

"At least a week, till we get somebody else."

"How long will that be?"

"I don't know."

I made him an offer: "It's not working sixteen hours a day. I work just eight hours on my days off on his schedule. So three days I'd be working sixteen hours, and the other two days eight. Why don't you let me take his schedule, and I'll take it for the whole month of August?"

"You would? That would sure be nice, if you don't mind."

I explained that I could be putting my garden in, taking the kids fishing for a month, etc. But in the back of my mind, I'm saying, *Here's the overtime for me.*

I was scheduled to go to the Arizona Mission the second week of September, and I'd already scheduled that week for vacation.

When September came, he called me into his office again. "We'll take you off Orson's schedule, and you'll only have to work your schedule."

"I'm on vacation that week."

"I know that."

"What about that meeting we had about being given compensatory time for overtime?"

"Oh, yeah. Joe's got every hour you've worked, every shift."

"Would it be all right if I took some of that time off this fall or winter?"

"No, we'd rather you take it off when we don't have vacations, which is to our advantage too. Go see Joe. Let him work that out for you."

He told Joe, "Let this guy have a couple of weeks when he wants them."

Joe asked me, "When do you want those weeks?"

I went home and looked at the schedule Dilworth Young had sent me. Then I went back to Joe and said, "I've got five weeks of overtime coming, plus my week of vacation—and that makes six weeks. I only need five. Can I have them?"

"That would work perfect," Joe said.

So I started working overtime.

The next year, I ended with some more missions: the Colorado, Washington DC, and Boston Missions. Now I would have to take off a week or two at a time. Later, I was given the Canada Halifax Mission, which included all the Maritime Provinces, two or three thousand miles wide, which had no stakes.

Then I was called to be a regional representative, with a dual capacity. I was also called to serve on the Missionary Committee of the Church. But I never missed a meeting, because I always had overtime.

I learned that the First Quorum of the Seventies was going to be reorganized. A letter from Spencer W. Kimball, now president of the Church, explained, "You're to take your last trips into the missions in Canada, and then report. You'll be released at October general conference."

September came again, and the management at Geneva called another meeting at the old Vineyard church. The superintendent got up and said, "Well, Gentlemen, you haven't been paid for overtime in the past, and you're not going to be paid for it now. But the last two years, we've been giving you a compensatory hour for every hour you worked overtime. As of the first of October, that will be discontinued. These are the rules made by the corporation. I'm sorry. I hate to tell you that, but that's the way it is."

The compensatory hour policy had been initiated the month before I began traveling as a mission representative, and it was cancelled the day I was released. In my opinion, that was God's way of taking care of the problems associated with my traveling, though there's no way God will come down and sign an affidavit to that effect.

On one of my first assignments to Arizona, I was terrified. I'd never been anything but a stake missionary and an elders quorum president, and now I had to go meet with stake and mission presidents, many of whom had been prominent in their communities and big shots in companies. I was just a little hick from the sticks of American Fork, Utah.

Dewitt Paul was the mission president in the California Mission. He'd been a patriarch in New Jersey, and was the chief executive officer and chairman of the board of a Fortune 500 Company. But he had written me about a particular problem in the mission. I thought that those problems had to go up the ladder to the Brethren, but in my oral report to Dilworth Young and LeGrand Richards, they hadn't given me answers to the problem. They simply told me that the next time I went to the mission, the Lord would help me solve the problem.

Still, I worried about it, and President Paul worried about it. So three days before I went to the mission, I went to the temple twice and fasted both days. President Paul met me at the airport with his assistants.

We started to have zone conferences, and the problem lay heavy upon both of us. He and I, his wife and the mission staff talked at length about it, but we still had no answer. This left me feeling very inadequate. Still, President Paul insisted, "We've got to solve this problem while you're here."

We'd been up to Lompoc, and President Paul drove an exchange car back, while the assistants to the president took the new one. As we were driving on the freeway, President Paul said, "When you get to the Santa Monica Boulevard exit, just turn off." It would take us right to the mission home. We turned off and kept going and going.

Pretty soon we ended up right in the middle of Watts. I said to the president, "We're in the wrong place." By now, it's about one o'clock in the morning, and just then the red lights of a police car flashed. I pulled up to the officer and rolled my window down. When he saw two white guys in the car, he said, "What are you guys doing down here? You'll be dead in the morning. Don't you know this is Watts?!"

I confessed, "We're lost."

"You sure are!"

We followed him back onto the freeway, and he told us how to get back to the temple.

We were supposed to be at another zone conference which required us to be up about 5:30 or six o'clock, our last zone conference, the one where the problem existed.

That morning, as I crawled in bed, I offered a prayer: "Lord, we've got to solve this problem tomorrow, and I still don't have a solution. When I return to Salt Lake City, I've got to give a report. The Brethren will want to know what I did about the problem.

"And not only that, I've got to have a couple of hours sleep before our early morning zone conference. I've got to get some kind of answer."

Then the thought came to me, *The angels are supposed to help me. When I was set apart, I was told that the angels would help me.*

Just about that time, a kind of light came through the window, and I thought it was shining off the temple or it was a spotlight. (The mission home where I was staying is right next to the temple.) It kind of shone in the room and lit it up. It wasn't a bright light, like the sun, but it was a light.

All of a sudden, I could see an open book, like the scriptures, sitting on a hand. The top of the page of the book read "Chapter 59," and the verses "58 and 59." The book was something I'd never read before in all my reading, and I was allowed to read just the two verses.

As soon as I read the verses, the hand disappeared and the light faded, but they were the answer to my question for the next day. I fell right to sleep, and I don't think I've ever slept more soundly for maybe two and a half hours. When I woke up, I was alert and felt no tiredness at all. The scripture in D&C 84:80 reads, "He that doeth the works of righteousness shall not be weary in body, spirit, or mind." That day, I knew for a fact the truth of that promise.

When we arrived at the zone conference, I told President Paul, "I know for a fact that the problem will be taken care of today. I know what we're supposed to do."

We met quite a number of missionaries that morning, one of them a zone leader, a good missionary who had just a few months left on his mission. President Paul had almost called him to be his assistant.

We thought the problem was associated with something which in fact it wasn't. It was associated with the elder who was the zone leader.

We had long meetings in which the missionaries bore their testimonies, and when the zone leader stood up with the other leaders in his zone, he said, "All you people are lying. You all say the Church is true, but it's a lie. You don't know it's true. There's no spirit here."

Then his eyes began to roll back in his head, as if they were trying to hide behind the front of his cranium. President Paul looked at me, and I looked at him. I said, "This is the problem, and we'll take care of it right now." The elder continued to rant, evidence that he was not himself.

Several of us thought the missionary was possessed of the devil, but I stood up and said, "Will you all please be quiet for a moment."

I invited the elder to come forward, and as he did, his whole countenance became dark, such that even his skin seemed to change color. We set him on a chair, and President Paul, the assistants to the president, and I administered to him with oil. In the name of the Lord, we commanded the spirits to leave.

The elder became completely docile. Then he broke out in a sweat and asked, "What happened to me?" He couldn't remember a thing from the last one or two days.

This happened in front of all the missionaries. We then spoke to the missionaries and read some scriptures. The problem had been solved, and we did it in the Lord's way, not by talking to the missionaries individually.

I next went to the California East Mission, where Gerald Nelson was the mission president. We'd had a great spiritual experience in Whittier just six months before, one of the most spiritual meetings I'd ever been in in my life, the kind of meeting in which missionaries resolve to increase their ability and work by three hundred percent.

On this latter visit, I learned of a missionary who was very troubled. He was saying such things as the Church was not true, and he wasn't doing the work. He was also flirting with girls and trying to go on dates. The elder's father was a stake president, and President Nelson was going to send the elder home. But the Brethren in Salt Lake City told the president to keep him in the mission, and so he did. Were he sent home, it would have brought disgrace upon the stake president father. That's when President Nelson phoned me.

The elder had been acting up for six months, and now the other missionaries were angry with him and wanted to get rid of him. The missionaries and the zone leader were telling him that when Elder Pedersen came, he would straighten him out. "He'll be inspired to tell you exactly what's wrong with you. Just you wait till Elder Pedersen comes!"

After the zone conference ended, we met for some lunch. The assistants to the president came to me and said that Elder So-and-so was going to ask me a question, and "you'll be inspired to give him the right answer."

I looked at them and asked, "What's going on here? You should never have put me on the spot like that."

"Well," they explained, "we didn't find out about your coming till last night."

After all the missionaries had left, I walked down the aisle to where this one elder and about four others were waiting. I looked at the elder and said to myself, *Dear Lord, we are in bad trouble. I am not inspired. I don't know what to say. I don't know anything about this elder, and he doesn't know anything about me.*

The elder stopped me and said, "Elder Pedersen, these missionaries tell me you are inspired."

"Well, sometimes I am and sometimes I'm not."

Then he asked me a doctrinal question. I stopped, pointed my finger at him, and said, "Elder, this is the problem with you." And then I began to talk to him.

All the missionaries with him began to cry.

The elder confessed, "There's no way on earth you could have known those things about me except by the Spirit."

He later stopped me on the way to our meal and said, "I want to tell you what just happened. I'm going to be a different missionary from now on." And he did turn out to be a good missionary.

I had many experiences like that one.

One experience was unique. On my last visit to the California Mission, many of the missionaries were brought to me because they were sick. The many good doctors in Los Angeles took care of the missionaries for nothing, so if an elder had some chronic health problem, he'd be sent to one of those doctors.

Some sixteen missionaries lived in the mission home, where a good old lady from the South, a member of the Church, cooked for them. There was also a grand piano in a room where firesides and other gatherings could be held. So instead of going to a zone conference, President Paul and I would sometimes just sit around and talk to the missionaries who lived in the mission home.

President Paul felt that some of the missionaries weren't sick at all, including the secretary to the mission and some of the president's assistants.

PROPHECY FULFILLED

The previous Sunday, after we'd held a missionary meeting in Long Beach, two missionaries in that area began asking questions they were having difficulty with. In the zone meeting, as I stood to speak, I said, "Elder Crapo, from New Mexico, is going to tell you about his family."

I'd never met Elder Crapo before, but I told him he had a brother who had long hair and didn't want to go on a mission. I said to him, "When this meeting is over, you write him a letter," plus some things he was to say to his brother.

The gist of the situation is that two or three weeks later, he did write his brother and told him to get ready to accept a call on a mission. Three weeks later, I received a letter from the brother, thanking me for what I had told his missionary brother to write. Both elders later came to see me when the younger brother went to the MTC.

That afternoon in the mission home, President Paul said to me, "Elder Pedersen, I want you to talk to these missionaries." I opened the scriptures and started talking. I did not remember what I said until two and a half years later while I was in the temple. A young Elder Johnson was going on a mission, and the temple presidency was instructing him and other elders before they left on their missions. Such instructions usually focus on the wearing of the garments and keeping covenants, and usually the instructions last at most only ten minutes.

I asked Elder Johnson, "Where are you going on your mission?"

His father asked me, "Do you remember me? I was in that last meeting in the mission home in the Los Angeles Mission when you came on your last trip there."

"You were? Who else was there?"

He started naming them: Elder Woods, one of the assistants to the president, from Canada, and so on. Then he explained, "I'd like to tell everybody what happened, because tonight is the fulfillment of a prophecy."

I couldn't remember a thing.

"That night, you began to talk using the scriptures. Then you looked at each missionary and gave a kind of individual prophecy for each one. I've kept track of these prophecies over the years, and everything you told them has come true. I was the last missionary you addressed, and you said to me, 'Elder Johnson, I will not see you again until you send your son on a mission. I will be there.' Now you're here, and you are in the temple presidency. I had told my family, 'Brother Pedersen will be there.'"

OSCAR MCCONKIE

When I was a mission representative, I visited Arizona, where Oscar McConkie was the mission president. He did some things that other mission presidents couldn't do, because he was a McConkie. When the new missionary discussions came out, he called an all-district, three-day conference—like a general conference. This was to take place in March, before April general conference.

I said to him, "Oscar, that's not—"

"Well, I'm going to do it. I've got my brother Bruce coming down." Then he named other General Authorities who were going to be speakers at his conference.

Who was I to stop him? So I backed off.

Then he called me and said, "I want you to come down and speak for two hours on Thursday, an hour on Friday, and two hours on Saturday"—three talks.

"Oscar, I'm not coming. I'm only authorized to come when the Brethren say I can come. I was in your mission last month. I'm not going to break the rules."

He still insisted that I come down. He started calling me every two or three days, wanting to know what I was going to talk about.

Finally, I said to him, "Look, Oscar, if you've got General Authorities coming, I'm not coming. I'm a nobody. I'm not going to embarrass myself by speaking with General Authorities present. I don't mind talking to the missionaries—I don't mind doing that."

The conference was going to start on a Thursday, and he called me on Monday: "Are you coming?"

"No, I'm not coming, unless I'm told to by the Brethren."

"Okay," he replied. "I'll call you right back."

Five minutes later S. Dilworth Young called me: "Brother Pedersen, I'm authorizing you to go to Arizona."

I'd no sooner hung up the phone when Oscar McConkie called. "Well, I hear you're coming."

I wasn't angry, just a little frustrated. My thought was, "Man, that guy!"

"What are you going to speak about?" he wanted to know.

"Oscar, I don't know what I'm going to speak about. But I'll tell you what I'd like to do. I've been a stake missionary. I've been an elders quorum president. I've been on a stake high council. I've been a seventies president. I haven't been a bishop or in a stake presidency. There's one thing I *can* do."

"What's that?"

"You've put pressure on me to come, and I'm coming. Now I want you to do something. I want you to send some of your missionaries out tracting. Between now and Friday, have them find me a man who's willing to read the Joseph Smith story and nothing else. Have him agree to come and stand before your body of missionaries. Then I will demonstrate how the Holy Ghost will witness to that man that the gospel's true."

"That would be great," he said.

I added, "Send your missionaries out, but I want a man, not a woman."

My thought now was, "That'll take care of old Oscar," and I never thought any more about it.

I left work at four in the afternoon and drove half way through the night to be in Arizona at five o'clock in the morning. The mission conference was scheduled for eight o'clock in the morning, and lo and behold, Bruce R. McConkie had called and said he was not coming. So Oscar had typed up an agenda, just like at general conference, and he had assigned me to speak in Bruce R. McConkie's place.

I was very uptight.

I had brought my wife and two children down with me, and we stayed with my mother- and father-in-law, who'd gone to Arizona for the winter. They also came to hear me speak.

I stayed the rest of the day with Oscar and his missionaries and listened to the other speakers.

Then Oscar announced, "We've got a man for you."

"Well, good. I don't want to know anything about him. I don't even want to meet him till we get him in front of the missionaries."

"Why's that?"

"That's the way missionary work is. If you go knock on someone's door, what do you know about the person who answers? The Holy Ghost will witness to this man that the Church is true. That's all I need to know about him. If you tell me something about him, you'll probably scare me off."

President McConkie said, "Okay."

Friday morning we heard two or three speakers in a wonderful conference, followed by a big noon meal. The rich people in Maricopa County, fourteen stakes of them, donated a steak dinner for 240 missionaries—I'd never seen such a banquet for so many people in my life. The food just disappeared!

Oscar allowed a two-hour break, then gave me two hours to speak and do my demonstration. "Are you sure you don't want to know this guy?"

"No, I don't want to know anything about him."

"Well, two missionaries have tracted him out and brought him here."

The missionaries brought him to the stand, his wife with him. "This is Brother Vincent McMurrow," they announced.

I shook the hands of the couple and said, "God bless you. Welcome. This is going to be a wonderful day for us."

Oscar conducted the meeting. We had a song and a prayer, and then the man was introduced to the group. He turned out to be a retired Methodist minister.

I looked at the missionaries. I looked down at my wife, my daughters, and my in-laws. And my heart fell. I prayed, *Lord, I have really put you on the spot. I'd like to apologize right now. But there are 240 young men out there. Here's a retired Methodist minister.* (He was still being introduced.) *I have promised that the Holy Ghost would witness to him that the Church is true. I had no right to do that, but I've done it. For the sake of these 240 missionaries, and for the sake of this man's soul, you're going to have to forgive me and help me today. I don't deserve help, but this couple does. Please overlook my mess-up and take care of me one more time.*

The man was now standing on my right. "Brother McMurrow," I said, "you're a retired minister."

"Yes."

"Would you say something to these young men?"

He spoke for about two minutes while I stood by him, something about his ministry and what he'd done.

My old heart was heavy. Again I prayed, "Lord, I've got to have some help here."

On my mission to Denmark, we didn't have any set lessons, but I had prepared one special lesson. I'd read the first fifty pages or so of Orson Pratt's works, where he wrote about Joseph Smith in a way that I'd never heard before.

"Brother McMorrow, you have read this story of Joseph Smith. It sounds like a fairy tale, doesn't it? It's a remarkable story."

"That's true," he agreed. "If that story is true, it's got to be one of the greatest things that ever happened in history."

"Well, that's what I want to talk to you about. I myself believe it's true. All these young men and women here believe it's true. But you're a retired Methodist minister, so you don't believe it's true."

"That's right. I don't believe it."

"But the Holy Ghost is going to witness to you that it *is* true. I would like you to start reading the Joseph Smith story. As you read, if you don't mind, I'll interrupt you here and there along the way, not to be rude, but to emphasize something from the scriptures."

"Okay, we'll do that," he said.

So he started to read the Joseph Smith story. When he came to the place where Christ and God the Father appeared to Joseph, I interrupted: "Now, Brother McMurrow, did you know that the apostle Peter prophesied that that would happen?"

"No."

"Would you like to read that prophecy?"

"I'd be interested in that."

So we turned to Acts 3:19-21, where it says that the heavens must receive Christ until the restitution of all things. I read him those verses, then said, "Christ is now dead, and the heavens will receive him until the time of restitution of all things—so that has to be a time other than his crucifixion."

He agreed.

I continued: "If Peter said Christ was going to come, He'll be in heaven until there's a time of restitution. Christ will be coming back to earth, and something will be restored."

"That's right," he said.

"Do you know of any other church, other than what Joseph Smith founded, which teaches that Christ came and restored anything?"

"No."

Then the minister talked a little about John the Baptist, from Matthew 17:1-12. John as Elias would come and restore all things. Again, I asked if he knew of any church that claimed John the Baptist would come as prophesied by Christ. He said he didn't.

I'd been teaching this doctrine to nonmembers for forty years.

Eventually, we began talking about the Book of Mormon. I quoted to the minister from Ezekiel 37, and then about the Balfour Act, which established the land of Israel.

Finally, I said, "Brother McMurrow, there's no sense in going any further. The Holy Ghost is witnessing to me now that it has already witnessed to you that The Church of Jesus Christ of Latter-day Saints is true."

"That's the case," he confirmed. "I would like to be baptized into this church."

Oscar had timed the dialog—sixteen and a half minutes.

"Thank you, Brother McMurrow," I said. "Would you now please go over and sit down?" By now, his wife was crying—not with sorrow, but about how the Spirit had got hold of her and wrenched her heart. I was now crying myself.

I addressed the elders and sisters: "This is the way conversion happens." I turned to D&C 100 and read them verses 5 through 8, where elders are counseled, "For it shall be given you in the very hour, yea, in the very moment, what ye shall say" (also D&C 5:16).

"You simply bear your testimony," and that's what I did.

"Brother McMurrow, I bear you my testimony in the name of Jesus Christ that the Spirit has witnessed to you the truth of the restored gospel."

I turned again to the elders: "This is the pattern the Lord has set in the scriptures, and this pattern also applies to home teaching. President Harold B. Lee once said (p. 1057 of the December 1964 *Improvement Era*), "Home teaching means watching over the Church as the scriptures have defined it. Home teaching is nothing more than missionary work to those who are not members and to those who are members of the Church."

About half an hour had now passed, so I announced, "This meeting is adjourned."

President McConkie asked, "What are we going to do now?"

"That's up to you. You're the mission president."

He called some missionaries to come forward and speak, because he didn't want them leaving early. That would have been anti-climactic—after their seeing this minister being taught and converted the way he had been.

By the way, Brother McMorrow was baptized the next Friday.

Since then, whenever I meet missionaries from that time, that's all they remember of me; they don't remember anything else I ever said or did, even though I'd been in that mission on and off for three years.

I don't think what I did was courageous; it was just audacious. I'd been hoping the missionaries would bring in someone from off the street who had never gone to a church. That's the kind of people I usually had ended up talking to. Yes, I was bold, but I just do whatever comes to my mind.

Chapter Sixteen

New Zealand Mission President

I had some wonderful experiences when I was mission president in New Zealand, which show how the Sprit works with people. We can help people by giving them good advice, and when they act on it, they develop faith.

In the town of Rotorua, an Elder from Preston, Idaho, had been called by the stake president to serve as the elders quorum president in the Rotorua Ward. The ward "ship" was in bad shape. Another missionary, the elder's companion, served as the Young Men's president in the ward. The young people in the ward responded enthusiastically to the elder. Inactive members started coming out, and this elder asked if I'd be willing to help them.

The young people began to drive up to the mission home from Rotorua on a calendared day once a month, some fifty or sixty of them. My wife Shirley would make treats for them, and we'd hold a kind of fireside. In addition, some twenty-five to thirty nonmembers began to come along, so every time we went to Rotorua to have a zone conference, here would be all these nonmembers. We'd let them come to the conference and even bear their testimonies. Sometimes we held a baptism right after the conference.

THE STORY OF BUNTY

The ward was now going in a good direction. One young Maori girl in her early twenties came to the fireside two or three times. She was a devout member of the Assembly of God church, and she never missed one of its meetings. The elders set a baptism date for her, and they invited me to come down. Well, you can't go to every baptism in a mission field that's eighteen hundred miles long, so I said I wouldn't be able to come.

Monday was P-day, and I was in my office reading mail and getting caught up on things. The senior companion in Rotorua phoned, and he was in tears: "I've got some bad news. She's not going to be baptized."

I asked what was the matter.

"She was downtown and bumped into the Assembly of God minister, who wanted to know why she hadn't been to church for the last four or five months. She told him she was going to be baptized into the LDS Church on Wednesday.

"'Oh, they're the church of the devil,' he told her, and then told her many other things. Within a couple of days, he got all the faithful members of his church to convince her that the LDS Church was the church of the devil. She asked the elders to come and get her Book of Mormon; she didn't want to see the missionaries again. So he asked me, 'What do I do?'"

I told the elder to baptize her on Wednesday just the same. "When something like that happens, what we do or say won't matter. There's no way we can convince her that we are not the church of the devil. We'll just turn her over to the Lord."

"What?!" Elder Bennett asked.

"You just turn that kind of people over to the Lord. You and your companion start fasting right now, and my wife and I will also begin to fast. I'll get the AP's to fast, and we'll ask the office people also to fast. You go right over tonight and get that Book of Mormon."

It was then about 10:30 in the morning. I added, "We'll fast until tomorrow morning, and the baptism will still be on. You tell her that you'll be glad to take the Book of Mormon back, but not until she agrees to make a commitment to pray one more time and ask God if the Church is true. If she'll make that commitment, you take the Book of Mormon and go home. Your baptism will still be for Wednesday. Do you understand that?"

"Yes."

"There's another thing you might do. Call the other twelve missionaries in Rotorua to fast with you."

He wasn't able to reach them, but the rest of us had the fast. The elders went over and asked this sister to pray one more time. She said she didn't need to ask, so it all came down to whether she was going to pray again or not. Finally she said, "I'll pray one more time, but understand that I am making that commitment just to get rid of you. I don't want you around here anymore because I know you're the church of the devil."

The next morning, Elder Bennett phoned and said, "She's going to be baptized Wednesday."

"That's wonderful," I said.

The sister had told the Elders what happened:

Before I went to bed about 10:30 or 11:00, I knelt and prayed. I said, "Lord, I'm praying because I promised the elders that I'd pray and ask one more time if the Church is true. I know it's not. I know it's the church of the devil, but I've got to keep my promise, even if it's to people who are of the devil."

So I prayed and asked if the Church of Jesus Christ of Latter-day Saints was really true, and if so, I would be willing to join it. I was going to be baptized, but then I found out that it's the church of the devil.

Suddenly my room filled with light, and someone was standing there. All the person said was to read Exodus 3:16, Hebrews 12:4, and Revelations 1:3. I hurried up and wrote those numbers down, and as I wrote, the personage, whoever it was, was gone as fast as he had appeared. I was now excited. Somebody had told me to read what was an answer to my prayer.

Herschel and Shirley Pedersen.

Exodus 3:16 reads, "Call the elders of Israel." She got to thinking, *Who are the elders of Israel.* The only ones she knew were the Mormon elders, and the other missionaries who came to church.

The next line read, "And tell them the Lord God of Israel has appeared unto you." Tears came to her eyes, and she knew then that the personage who had come to her had to be Jesus.

Hebrews 12:4 reads, "The word of God is sharper than a two-edged sword to divide asunder both marrow and bone and joint and sinew." She knew that to be true. She knew that if she joined the

Church, her family and all her friends from the Assembly of God church would no longer speak to her.

The verse in Revelations said, "Blessed is he who reads the words of the prophecy." To her that meant that blessed is the person who reads the Book of Mormon.

At one in the morning she was till awake, thinking about what had happened to her. What did she do but call the elders and say, "Elder, I'm going to be baptized Wednesday."

Many remarkable things like that happened to us.

FASTING AND PRAYER

There was an inactive member of the Church in Murupara, married to a Rastafarian minister. When the missionaries visited her to try to get her to come to church, she explained that she would love to be active, but she wasn't going to divorce her husband (his ministry was their livelihood) and she wasn't going to cause trouble with her nonmember family.

The stake president of the Rotowa Stake would go to Murupara a couple of days a week, and he wanted to build a chapel there, because there were many inactive members in the area. So we sent four missionaries to Murupara, among them an elder, a Maori and also an outstanding athlete. Many of his relatives there were among the inactives.

Those people started to come to church, and within about five months, attendance at meeting rose from about twenty-five to about seventy-five. Papers were submitted, and they were allowed to build a chapel. Chapels in the mission field at that time were built in phases—first phase, second phase, and so on.

A variety of authorities, including the Church Real Estate Department, visited the area, and in the meantime, missionaries and the active members were talking to this sister, who was related to a number of the members.

Elder Allred told Sister Fara, "Look, if you want to be active in the Church, then pray. Tell the Lord that you want your husband to join the Church, and he'll join. It might take awhile, but he will join, and you will be married in the temple."

She agreed to begin doing that.

She fasted and prayed, as did her Maori relatives and the missionaries. In the meantime, the Church bought a beautiful little piece of ground to build a chapel on.

One day, this elder happened to visit this sister, and the old minister was home. He shook their hand cordially and invited them in. Then he asked them, "Do you believe in visions?"

"Yes, we believe in visions."

"Do you believe in dreams?"

"Yes."

He did not know that the Church had bought ground for a chapel. He continued, "In a dream, I saw people start to build a building on that piece of ground up there. And it looked like it was going to be a church. I saw inside the building and everything. Somebody's going to build a church up there."

The elder confirmed that, "That's us. We're going to build a church there."

"What?" the minister exclaimed.

A few months later, when ground was broken, the minister, his wife, and the family walked to the site. When it came time to dedicate the chapel, Glen Rudd, the Area President, came. We had invited the mayor, the city council, and the town's ministers to the dedication.

Fifteen minutes before the meeting, the minister walked through the building, tears in his eyes. Then he said, "This is exactly what I saw months ago before even a shovelful of dirt was taken from this site. I saw all this!"

After the dedication, the old minister came up and asked, "What do I have to do to be baptized? This is where I belong."

We told him, "The elders will take care of that." He took the lessons and in about three weeks was baptized.

About a week before he was baptized, he attended his church. His wife and family were there. He stood and said, "I've been your minister for a long time. Everything has been right and good in this church. But I have learned that I have not belonged to the true church. I've found the only true church approved by God. My wife and family are going to be baptized into The Church of Jesus Christ of Latter-day Saints."

Then he related the dream he had had. "I would like you all to come down and see me baptized. I don't know what I'm going to do for a living. I'll have to depend on the Lord for that."

A family in that congregation invited the missionaries to come to their home. So Elder Cornell taught the gospel to this large Maori family. The missionaries gave each member of the family a Book of Mormon.

When the father received his Book of Mormon, he said, "I've never had a book given to me. I've never owned a book in my life, but the sad thing is, I can't read."

The elders offered, "We'll come and start teaching you to read." The father, now very grateful, began to cry, just thinking that the missionaries were going to try to teach him and his wife to read.

When he went to bed that night, he put his Book of Mormon under his pillow. Realizing that this book was about his own people, he knelt down and offered a prayer. As he read the title of the book, it was as though every letter was on fire, the flames rising from the letters, but they didn't burn the book. He woke his wife, and she saw the same thing.

With the help of the missionaries, he finally was able to read the Book of Mormon, and he was baptized.

THE ENGLISH MINISTER

We also baptized an elderly English minister, Charles Forbes, who was a Maori, and his wife. Brother Forbes had been the head minister of the Apostolic Church in Auckland for some fifty years. He knew his Bible upside down and backwards.

Some of his wife's relatives were members of the LDS Church, and one of them, a great Maori (even though he had been excommunicated from the Church, but had now been re-baptized; I went on trade-offs with him), asked us to visit the minister. We reactivated him in a fifteen-minute conversation.

The minister was seventy-eight years old at the time, so he had retired, though he attended his church regularly. As we began talking to him, he said, "I'd like to ask you some questions. I've read and preached the Bible, but there are a lot of things in it that are not clear. One of them has to do with the lost tribes of Israel, and how they were to begin again to receive the sacrament of the bread and water."

We visited this minister about every three weeks and became good friends with him. Pretty soon we were getting ready to baptize Charlie and his whole family, except for one daughter who, with her two children, was living with him. She was also living with a guy, so we couldn't baptize her. I told her that she needed to pray: "You pray and ask the Lord how bad it will be on the other side if you don't live a moral life here and join the Church." We went ahead with the family's baptism, all except the daughter.

Then Charles Forbes got cancer. We were able to seal him and his wife in the temple, but then he passed away. That kind of shook up the daughter. About two or three days after her father's funeral, she had a vision. She got to thinking about how bad it would be in the next life if you weren't a member of the Church.

Her sixteen-year-old daughter was as immoral as her mother, but she also had a vision in which she thought her spirit left her body. She found herself in a very dim place, where there were millions and millions of people, all with hideous looks of pain and anguish, all screaming, "Please help me! Please help me!"

Further along, she could see a little light, as if she were going into a tunnel. She asked the people, "Why can't you get out?"

"Because we were adulterers, murderers, and thieves in life. Please help us, and don't end up like we are."

The vision terrified the daughter.

"What are you going to do?" I asked her.

"Well, I've got to change my life."

I don't know whatever happened to her.

PUKUHONÉ WARD

Every Tuesday night, we would drive to Pukuhohé, a city of about 25,000 people, to visit the big ward there. I would take my assistants, and we would do "splits" with the two missionaries working there.

As we visited, the ward grew quickly. The ward mission leader would make assignments, and the bishop would call and tell us how many visits we were to make.

One night we came across a sister who hadn't been to church for some twenty years. Her husband, once the bishop, had been excommunicated, and she had never returned to church meetings after he died. I asked her, "How come you don't come to church?"

"Aw," she said, "there ain't no sense in me going to church. My husband was excommunicated before the temple was built in Hamilton. We were getting ready to go to the temple, but then he was excommunicated for immorality. I can't be sealed to him, and I don't want to be sealed to anybody else. He's in hell on the other side, and I'll be in hell with him."

I said to her, "Sister Thompson, I believe something can be done about this. Why don't you get your genealogy ready?"

"It's all done. It's in boxes under the bed."

"In boxes?" I asked, surprised.

"Yeah, I left it there. I haven't taken it out since the day my husband died. Ain't no sense in doing it. My husband can't be a member no more, and I can't go to heaven."

I explained, "There's a way that God can forgive people. There's a way you can be sealed to him. There's got to be a way. God isn't cruel. Your husband has been living in hell for all these years, wanting to have his work done.

"I'll tell you what we'll do. You fast and pray, and I'll fast and pray with you. You come to church on Sunday. We'll come back next week and see how you feel about everything."

She said, "Okay."

When I met with her the next Tuesday, I asked her, "Did you pray?"

"Yup. I fasted and prayed, and my husband come and stood right there at the foot of my bed. He told me to get the boxes out, and get the family history people in the ward to help me."

"We've got to get the stuff together, and you've got to get the work done, so you can be sealed to me. The rules sometimes change, and I want us to be sealed. I'm over here waiting to have my work done. You get my work done."

I asked her what she was going to do about it all.

"Oh, he's made me wait these many years. Now I'm going to make him wait." She was just an ornery old Maori lady, in her eighties. "I'll be going to church all the time. I'm going to get myself ready to go to the temple."

"Well, how long are you going to make your husband wait?"

"Until I think he's paid the price for stepping out on me."

"Sister, you've got to forgive him."

"I forgave him a long time ago, but if I'm going to be sealed to him, he's got to pay the price."

I told her I didn't even know how long it took to get papers approved. "We'll start preparing the papers, and it will be at least a year before you can go to the temple."

She said she'd start getting ready.

I called the area president and posed my problem: "There's a man who was a bishop who was excommunicated. I've told his wife we can get him rebaptized somehow, and she could be sealed to him in the temple. He was excommunicated before there was a temple in New Zealand."

"Boy, I don't know about that," he replied. "That's never been done that I know of. Still, we'll write everything up."

We wrote up all the information and sent it to the Area President. He said he'd send the papers to the First Presidency's office and let them make the decision.

About six months later, this sister announced to me, "I've thought about it, and I'll be sealed to my husband in a year."

I said, "Okay."

The Area President said he'd get a letter off to the First Presidency.

About three or four weeks later, he called to say that no decision had yet been made in the matter. Such permission had never been allowed before.

I still felt there had to be some way to get this situation resolved.

About four or five days before this sister's year was up, she called me: "Where's the papers. Where's the permission. I'm ready to go to the temple."

I phoned the bishop and asked if he could delay her for a week or two. Then I called the Area President: "This sister is ready to go to the temple. Her family are now active in the Church. The kids are saying, 'If Papa can be a member, we can all be sealed. We're going to do the temple work for all the names in these boxes, the names we've been gathering since before 1958.'"

A couple of weeks passed. The bishop said, "I can't hold this sister off any longer."

I told him, "Go ahead and give her a recommend. Tell her to go to the temple with the children and take their endowments out. We still don't have permission from the First Presidency to rebaptize her husband."

It had now of course been more than a year since we submitted papers, and we had a new Area President. I told him, "If she and the children can't be sealed, just tell me, so I can be the one to tell her."

He consented to call the First Presidency again.

He phoned me the next morning: "Brother Pedersen, Church policy has been changed. I've told the Brethren the circumstances, and they have talked about it many times. I've been instructed to have you fill out the man's papers as though he had never been a member of the Church. Show him as being endowed as a nonmember. Have the clerk destroy the excommunication papers, and then proceed with the ordinance work."

About two or three weeks later, we received the official letter through the Area President.

HEMI

Two nights before I was baptized, Sister Matthews, Sister Bates, Tonya and I drove to the visitors' center to watch some of the video on smoking. During the video clip, we talked about Joseph Smith and the Holy Spirit. When the video ended, he closed with a prayer. Tonya and the sisters drove me home.

When I arrived home, I felt as though another presence was in my bedroom. I knelt down and began to pray for help. And then the presence began to laugh. I recited part of the Lord's prayer—"Our Father which art in Heaven"—then quickly rushed from my room to find comfort from a friend, Manol, and I dragged him into my room. I left him in the room, then walked into his room.

After a minute or two, Manol appeared back in his room, where I was. He said, "Fetch, man, there's something wrong in your room."

At that point, I fled to the lake to pray for help. I walked through the gates to the lake. Everything around me stood still; everything was silent. When I knelt down and started to pray, I received a wonderful feeling. I felt my parents' presence, as well as that of the Holy Ghost—as if a big, strong hand was pushing on the back of my head, forcing my head to the ground.

When I finally raised my head from the ground, I saw a figure in front of me, and two other figures standing by his side. One of them, my father, said that it would be safest for me to be baptized. That's how I knew that being baptized would be my first step toward being able to live again with my parents and my Heavenly Father in the celestial kingdom.

When I heard my father's voice, I began to cry. I knew that my prayers had been answered.

I slowly rose and began to walk back home. As I looked toward the gate of the lake, I saw car lights coming past the gate, though I could hear nothing. I dashed toward the gate, and as I ran through it, everything around me returned to normal.

I continued running home, where I rang Sister Matthews to ask the missionaries to set a date for my baptism—immediately. She knew that something had happened.

This is my testimony. Here is my address. Come and see me, but bring your boxing gloves and a referee.

ANN WHITTER

Another story was typed up by a sister who was going to put it in a book, though whether she did or not, I don't know. Ann Whitter was a Maori girl who was inactive in the Church and was on drugs. She describes her experience when the prophets Ammon and Moroni visited her:

I stood on the beach, always at the same spot, praying as if I were a child. And it was always the same raceway dream. It was as though as time progressed, all the seafood diminished. I saw in a vision how those seafood beds could be replenished. My grandfather, now deceased, knew how to replenish them, and he had passed that knowledge down to my father. I had watched my father recite the same words, so that the abundance of seafood would return, if only for a brief period or season. Then the beds would again be empty.

Like unto a parable, my ancestors had been taught the truths of the saving gospel, and they had great faith in our Savior, Jesus Christ. But as time passed, they all strayed from those precious eternal truths, which had been replaced by false doctrines and the worship of idols. Only a total restoration could save us and bring many back into the fold of God.

The vision continued. My father's younger brother began to murmur. He wanted the power or gift of those precious words, though the time was not right for that. He was also not the one chosen.

I decided to take up the search down to the rocks, foraging for the key. To my astonishment, a young boy appeared, dressed in clothing and with hair of exquisite whiteness. He beckoned me: "Do you want to know the truth?"

"Yes," I replied.

"Come follow me," he answered, then moved off to a rock farther away. "Look," he added.

There, engraven in the bleached oyster shell, stood two elders, one with his right arm to the square. Amazed, I looked towards their identification badges, which bore the words "The Church of Jesus Christ of Latter-day Saints." They knew my ancestors would have fallen away, but also that a restoration would come. They could identify the missionaries, who traveled in pairs, raising their right arms to the square and wearing the Church's name.

The raising of the right hand to the square had come in a vision to the old Maori Chief in 1853. After the British occupied New Zealand, the Maoris wondered which church they should join. After this old chief fasted and prayed for eight days, he was told that the people of the true church would come from the east, they'd travel in twos, they'd wear identification badges, and they'd raise their right arm to the square when they prayed. This is what the old Maori saw who had been looking for seafood.

The story continues:

The missionaries had known my ancestors, who knew there'd be a falling away, but a restoration would come, and they'd know it when they saw the behavior of the missionaries. We read in Helaman 15:6 that the converted Lamanites strove "with unwearied diligence that they may bring the remainder of their brethren to the knowledge of the truth." That was part of the Father's Presentation—that the people would be restored to the knowledge of their fathers.

Now having received a personal testimony, I set about to collect items for my father's birthday, all the while being amazed at all that had happened. My grandfather had told my dad about his memory of those words. So how do I now undertake to unlock the door of my gift? First I look to the civilizing and understanding that the body needs to be nourished by the Spirit, and then I need to conclude by bearing my testimony. Because I had prayed fervently to my Heavenly Father, it was his will to send my grandfather back and tell me the words.

Again, these kinds of things happen. Many, many people had visions and dreams of these things. We have numerous accounts of them, and they've all been typed up. Glenn Rudd came to the mission because he'd been hearing about these things. Rumors get around. So we wrote them all up and gave him close to fifteen hundred such stories. We averaged between twenty-five and thirty a week. He said they'd all be put in a book someday. I have only a few excerpts, like abridgments, the basics of the stories.

When I began to hear them, the stories were so unusual I had the missionaries and the members write them down. In many cases, when the missionaries knocked on the door, the woman would say, "Yeah, I knew you were coming. It was made known to me this morning that you'd be knocking on my door." Then she'd invite them in.

ELDER COLEMAN

Elder Coleman, from Payson, Utah, was on the island of Aitutaki, where there lived a nonmember whose father had been a member, as well as an inactive man who held the office of teacher. These men were friends. They lived about seven kilometers from the chapel. One day Elder Coleman was at the church giving the "Father's Presentation" to the sixty-five-year-old inactive Church member, telling him that he needed to become active in the Church so he would be worthy someday to go to the temple, even though it was miles away. He could send his parents' names to the temple for their work to be done, and when he had saved up money, he could go to the temple and be sealed to them.

The old man didn't believe what the elder said. But the other old man, the nonmember whose father had been a member, told his friend, "You need to be baptized so you can be sealed to your father, who's already a member."

About a week later, Elder Coleman and his companion rode back to see these two men who were neighbors. The men reported, "Well, we've talked about it all an awful lot. We've talked about it every day. We thought we'd pray about it, and guess what? Both our fathers appeared to us and said, 'That's right. You need to be baptized so you can be sealed to me. You need to become active so that you can do my work and I can be sealed to you.' We've agreed that that's what we're going to do. We're going to start going to church."

Elder Coleman said, "Well, we'll see you at church on Sunday. It starts at this time."

"We'll be there," the gentlemen said.

THE JESSICA ELASH STORY

The story of Jessica Elash, a Maori girl, is one of the longest stories I have.

Jessica had become pregnant by a young man named Shane, and they married. The parents of both had hated each other, so the boy and girl would slip off into the bushes of the Marangi Bay area. They smoked, they drank, and he was an inactive member of the Church. They ended up with three children.

As the arm wrestling champion of New Zealand, the husband was invited to the World Championships in San Francisco, but the U.S. government would not grant him a visa, because he'd spent some time in jail as a felon.

Yet he would often say to his wife (when he wasn't drunk), "You ought to read the Book of Mormon someday," this even though he never went to church.

He also gambled, and he lost his job. The couple had relatives in Huntley who belonged to the Church. One of the women was a Relief Society president, and another the Young Women's president. When the couple visited there, members of the Church once in a while invited them to go to church and to firesides. Of course the couple refused.

Jessica had a brother named Harri, who had left the north country to live in Huntley, where he was trying to continue his education at Y Cottley University. (Maoris attend those universities free because they are native citizens of New Zealand—one of the benefits to minority groups.)

An Elder Sutherland had baptized Harri, and Harri had invited his family to the baptism. But the family hated the Church, so none of them went to the baptism. Then Harri, when he came to a zone conference, asked me what he could do to get his family baptized. There was also a young man who was preparing to go on a mission in a year. He was already going on splits with the missionaries.

I told Harri that if he'd he fast and pray once every week for his family, the Lord would open up a way for the family to join the Church. He indicated that the first family member he wanted to baptize was his sister Jessica, the wife of Shane.

I told him, "You invite your sister here, and get her husband and kids to come along. We'll get her baptized."

I let Elder Orth, the district leader at the time, and Elder Stutz know that Jessica was coming with her husband and kids. Jessica's relatives had guaranteed that if they'd come to a Sunday night fireside in a couple of weeks, Harri would speak at it. The Saturday before, there would be some type of activity at the Church—dancing and singing and other Maori types of things.

Jessica was all for that. But when she arrived at the dance, the first thing she said was "President Pedersen is not dressed in a way Mormons dress." That embarrassed her, and so she left the gathering.

The next day, all sorts of people were putting pressure on these nonmembers to go to the fireside. Jessica later admitted, "I tried to get sick. I tried everything. When the time came and my brother arrived, I was still in my pajamas."

He looked at me and said, "Look, we're going, even if we're late. I'm speaking tonight, and I'm your brother, and so you've got to come and hear me give my talk."

He was to be the first speaker, and everyone knew that the fireside was being held especially for Jessica and her husband.

My wife and I sat on the stand, and of course the couple was a little late. Harri gave his talk, while looking at his family and telling them how proud he was that they'd helped him join the Church, and how he was planning to go on a mission. Then he looked at his sister and said: "The Church is the only life for you, and I'd like you to consider it."

She only smiled at him.

When I got up to speak, I talked about a lot of things—my family, baptism, some scriptures out of the Book of Mormon, and so on. (Jessica, later in a long letter, said she had become caught up in my remarks.)

During refreshments afterwards in the cultural hall, I went up to Jessica and said, "Jessica, you felt the Spirit here tonight, didn't you?"

She admitted, "Yes."

"Well, then, when are you going to be baptized?"

Taken aback, she looked at me, then looked at her husband, Shane. He was the one who, although inactive in the Church, had said she ought to read the Book of Mormon once in a while.

My wife and I talked to Jessica for a while, then for about fifteen minutes went around and talked to the missionaries and others present. Jessica returned to talk to me, a smile on her face.

I looked at her, and at her cute kids, and said, "Look at all those cute kids. Someday they're not going to be yours. If you don't take them to the temple and have them sealed to you, they'll be taken away from you." I turned to Shane and said, "Shane, you're a member of the Church, so you know what I've just said is true."

Shane started to cry.

I continued: "I'll tell you what. We're going to arrange for your baptism next Saturday night, right here in Huntley. We'll teach you all the discussions in a week. Where do you live?" They lived in a trailer house up in the north country, with not even a branch or ward within fifty miles.

Shane wasn't so sure about that. He said, "No missionaries will come that far to teach the discussions." Shane was then out of work.

I told Elder Stutz and his companion to go up there the next day and begin teaching Jessica the missionary lessons.

Jessica and Shane went back down to Huntley on Thursday, where they listened to all the lessons again. On Saturday, we baptized Jessica. When we blessed her, we promised her that if she would live the gospel, her parents would join the Church.

Jessica started fasting and praying right away that her family would join the Church, and by the time we left our mission to come home, over fifty people in that family had come into the Church, all this because we had a little "Father's Presentation" in a fireside.

Two Other Experiences

Let me mention two other experiences, one of which I haven't written down.

We are foreordained in this life to do whatever we are supposed to do. I believe I was called to New Zealand because I had been foreordained to be there. The missionaries who came with me were also foreordained to be there. An experience of a dear friend of ours named Ida Medina will show what I mean. She wrote:

"It was the first week in December, a Saturday night. I had decided to go dancing with my sister. It was a time in my life when I felt that no one followed any of the teachings of Jesus Christ or his prophets. I felt alone in my beliefs and had settled with the way things were. In a world where people drank, smoked, and had meaningless sexual affairs, I didn't have in my spirit to do such things, so I would just make up silly reasons for not doing any of them. Many times I'd pray to my Father in Heaven, but my prayers always seemed hopeless. I'd go from church to church, but I never felt the Father there.

"This Saturday wasn't special. I went home and tried to ready myself for another week. I fell asleep quickly and had a dream. I was out dancing with my sister when a lady in white appeared in my room and stopped all the motion. I became frightened and ran behind a table to hide from her. She was wearing white and was about as tall as I am.

"She gracefully approached me, then took my hand. Although I didn't see her mouth move, I heard her speak. She made me feel safe and comforted. I followed her to the end of the room.

"The wall opened up and we walked through it into a field surrounded by people. We all walked together to a building filled with generous, caring people. I saw them working and helping each other. I saw a soup kitchen, classes, and many other things they were doing.

"Next, still holding my hand, she showed me a man in his early twenties, and he told me many things about himself—his childhood, his hobbies, even his home and the room he slept in. His given name was Ryan, and he told me he would give me something wonderful.

"Then the lady let go of my hand, and I awakened. I knew the dream was unusual, so I told my family about it. A month later, I saw a commercial about the Book of Mormon, so I called to ask to receive a copy. I was asked if I'd like representatives to visit me.

"I agreed, and four weeks later, the missionaries came to my door. They came in, sat down, and we exchanged names. When one of the missionaries said his name was Ryan, I couldn't believe it. I proceeded to ask him questions about his hobbies, and to my surprise, he was just as the lady had described them.

"After we talked awhile, Ryan was eager to know how I knew so much about him, but I was afraid to tell him. When I finally did tell

Recipients of the 2007 Emeriti Awards.
Front row, left to right: Robert W. Blair, William Grant Bangerter, Lera Benson Whittle, Elaine McAllister Moody, Maxine Petty Cameron.
Back row, left to right: George D. Durant, Herschel N. Pedersen, James E. Mangum, Allan B. Gomez, Mark G. Hathaway.

him, he explained that a person can receive 'personal revelation.' (The dream experience, by the way, had happened before he had arrived in the mission field.) I was happy to have the information.

"I visited the church and realized that it was the same building I had seen in my dream. The people there, their attitude, the way they taught, the soup kitchen, the classrooms—all were exactly as I had seen them.

"I was baptized a few months later. Since then I have received other messages and dreams for myself, and I know my Heavenly Father always loves me."

Sister Ida Medina is a lovely young lady. She had been married, had had a child, but was divorced when this story happened. She was looking for the true church, and she found it.

So I believe our lives have been planned, so to speak. Because we have our agency, we can change the plan—we can be disobedient, or we can become unworthy. I believe the Spirit works with people: "It goes over the land to prepare the hearts of the people to receive the gospel" (Alma 16:16). If I'm foreordained to do something in a certain place, and I do what I'm supposed to do, the Spirit will have me there when it's all supposed to happen, and everything will fall into place. I tried to teach the missionaries that principle.

We had sixteen Cook Islands in our mission. After a missionary had been in the mission three or four months, we'd have to fly him out to one of those islands on a little airplane, and the cost of that transportation was high. Thus if you put two elders on a remote island with two or three thousand people on it, you have to have elders you can trust; they've got to be faithful young men.

I sent Elder Howell, a big Maori kid, and Elder Smith to the island of Moki, where we had a small branch and a small chapel. Elder Howell had made the great sacrifice of a professional rugby career in Australia to go on his mission, something like $18,000 a month. (When the chapel was originally built by the Church, there were living quarters for the elders, connected to the chapel. The elders paid rent for their quarters.)

I sent Elder Howell simply because I felt he should go there, whether by inspiration or desperation—though I'd like to think it was inspiration. They had been there a little while when one night Elder Howell had a dream, or a vision. He saw his grandfather come to him, to tell him that the Maoris had come from the Cook Islands down to New Zealand. Not only that, the grandfather added that Elder Howell had Chinese blood in him. Chinese sailors had visited the island and stayed there for a while. As Elder Howell went around the island, he began to find some people who had known his grandfather.

We had on the island of Moki a kind of religion class, taught by a local man there. The Church Educational System had established little seminaries on the island, and the missionaries taught the classes in the evenings.

On these islands, there was no television, and hardly any radios. For activities, the people played volleyball and other sports, and they had spear-throwing contests, such as the natives have, as well as other activities. After the seminary classes, there would be these activities.

Elders Howell and Smith had dozens and dozens of young people coming to their classes and activities. The work was going very well.

One night, all of a sudden they saw a man looking in the windows of their quarters—a big man, over seven feet tall. Elder Howell, being the big man he was, said, "If you're out there when I come out, you'd better be gone, or I'll whip you!"

The elders went running out, but there was no one. When they returned inside, they decided it must have been an evil spirit—that's how missionaries think, you know. So they started praying for the Lord to protect them.

Then they looked outside again, and surrounding the building there were thousands and thousands of evil spirits trying to get into the chapel and their living quarters. That's when they called me on the phone. I told them, "Just have a little prayer and tell the Lord to ask the spirits to leave. Then they'll leave."

The incident with evil spirits happened more frequently. At the next activity with the young people, they had several people ready to be baptized. Elder Howell was in the shower, and Elder Smith in the room, when all of a sudden the large man came in. Just as Elder Howell came out of the shower, there stood this tall man, threatening them. Now they were really afraid.

They panicked and offered a quick prayer. All of a sudden, there were angels standing in the room with them, their swords drawn. The personage, whoever he was, disappeared.

I finally had to transfer the elders off the island, things got so bad, and we sent two other elders there. Why the elders had been permitted to see all the evil spirits and everything else, I don't know. But such things do happen to the missionaries once in a while.

We had a small missionary from Dunedin, Elder Gail, a very spiritual fellow. I sent him up to Whangarei, where there was an ex-bishop who had apostatized from the Church. Although Elder Gail didn't stand more than five feet, three inches tall and didn't weigh more than about 130 pounds, he was the cockiest, most arrogant little guy you ever saw in your life. He didn't mind telling anybody off, so I always had a little trouble with him, trying to calm him down.

He went to see this ex-bishop, a big Maori. He walked up to him and said, "You apostatized from the Church thirty years ago. I've come to tell you that you've got to get back into the Church. You've got to become active again."

Elder Gail would go back every week and pull the same tirade on the man. One day when he went, the man was on his porch. He said to the elder, "Get away from here. I don't want you ever here again. You're not welcome here."

When Elder Gail walked up to him, about to open his mouth, the man punched him smack in the face and knocked him off the steps and onto his back on the sidewalk. "Now will you get out of here?!"

By now, Elder Gail was a different elder. This is the day he began to change. He spoke up, "Sir, I'm sorry. But I came to tell you that I love you, and we need you in the Church. Won't you please come back?"

The old bishop started to come back in the Church.

We called this missionary "Railing Gail." When missionaries were about to go home, we'd take them to the temple for three days, where they'd do baptisms for the dead, endowments, and sealings. On the third day, we would have President Russon talk to them and let them ask questions about the temple. I had instigated this policy as a way to get the missionaries interested in continuing to go to the temple. (All my life I've been a fanatic about temple work.)

Elder Gail said,

"I went to the Lord's house and prayed my devotions to our God. There I had a vision in which I saw a sister missionary doing work on behalf of the dead. I pondered—how does the Lord accept this work? Do the dead accept it? In answer to my thoughts, my mind was opened. I saw thousands of people who had gone before us. I even saw this sister missionary meet her loved ones on the other side.' (This sister was also on her way home from her mission.)

"I also saw my deceased mother, and she was crying, but I didn't know why. The Spirit told me that I was to do her work, to make sure she was saved in the kingdom of God. I'm now doing research and studying to learn the things I must do."

MISSIONARY MISTAKE

Some missionaries in Whangarei had baptized two teenage Maori girls without getting permission from the very devout Catholic parents. The girl had told the missionaries that that was how it would have to be. So now the parents and the Catholic Church were very angry with our church, threatening a lawsuit to have the Church kicked out of New Zealand, along with the missionaries.

I arranged to meet the family so I could make things right with them and talk to them before they went ahead with the court case. I arranged for an excommunicated Maori to come with my wife and me. We also invited the Felts, couple missionaries, but no young elders. We fasted and prayed.

Talk about anger—it was not a pleasant situation to walk into. The father had been working the two girls over all morning, and when we arrived, they were crying. Then the father and mother began to unload on us. We had learned a long time ago just to let people get all the poison out, and then maybe you can get a little good in. When the parents were finished, I said to them, "Is there anything else you'd like to say? I'd like you to voice all your feelings and views right now, so that we can straighten this situation out in a peaceful manner."

They said a few more things, and we basically just listened. Then I spoke: "Look, I'm the president of the mission. I represent my church. I'm authorized to come to some kind of agreement with you. It looks like there are four or five things we can do. I know you want to sue my church and get us kicked out of New Zealand. I understand your point of view, and that's one option.

"The missionaries are young men, impulsive, and when you were young, you probably did a few things that probably weren't one hundred percent right. We sometimes do things that hurt other people's feelings."

The father agreed.

"That's another option—just allow that these young men made a mistake. There's another thing we can do: We can have your daughters' names removed from the records of our church, to show that they had never been baptized. But look at your daughters—would that make them happy? They want to be members of our church, right?"

The daughters agreed: "Yes, we want to be members."

"So it wouldn't make them happy if you sued our church," I observed. "I'd like to suggest a couple of other things."

"What's that?"

"First of all, you really don't know much about the LDS Church."

"That's right."

"You've never attended our meetings or read the Book of Mormon. We have Brother and Sister Felt here, a fine couple about your age. Could we have them come over, bring a Book of Mormon, and, with your girls sitting here, let them explain some of the things your daughters have been taught, so you can make a rational decision whether the LDS Church will have a bad effect on them. If you find something negative, something drastically bad, we'll take their names off the Church records. Please let your daughters remain members of our church until then. Your children would be very hurt if we took their names off the records right now.

"Another thing. As you know, the Catholic Church is very different from the LDS Church. Before we make a final decision, we would like to give you, your wife, and your children a blessing. We're supposed to hold the priesthood. As it says in the Bible, whenever you enter a house, "leave a blessing." You've received us today. When we came, you were a little hostile, but it now it looks like your anger has kind of disappeared. So we would like to leave a blessing on your house.

"You're the father, and you're the mother, and these are your children. I think you'd like your children to be happy, as well as you'd like to be happy.

"We have to make some kind of good decision. I suggest you put off the court case and take one of these other routes. What would you like to do?"

The father spoke: "I don't want my children to be members of your church, and I don't want to sue and cause a bunch of trouble and make my children unhappy. Their friends are all members of your church. You say you'd like to leave a prayer and blessing on our home?"

"I sure would."

"Why don't you do that?"

I said to him, "If you don't mind, we'd like to bless you first." We sat him down in a chair, and Brother Felt and I gave him a blessing. We told him that one day he would be a leader of the Church and have his family sealed together for eternity in the temple."

These were of course doctrines he didn't understand, but we told him the Felts would explain them to him.

We then blessed his wife, and as we did, the tears rolled down her cheeks. We blessed each of the girls, and then the whole family. The last family member was a boy about twelve years old. I said to the father, "Look at that little boy, a great young man." Then I asked the boy, "Would you like to have a blessing too?"

"Yeah," he said.

I asked the father, "Would you mind if we gave him a blessing?"

"No, give him a blessing."

I told the boy he would become a great athlete and be strong, as the Maoris want to be strong. I blessed him that someday he would join The Church of Jesus Christ of Latter-day Saints and go on a mission to Russia."

...*What did I just say?!* At that time, there were no missionaries in Russia.

When I finished the blessing, tears were running down the father's face. The father thanked us and asked the Felts if his family could come to church on Sunday. We knelt in prayer and then left the home. We'd been there about two and a half hours.

So the Felts began visiting them. When we left the mission, the family were all members of the Church.

We had hundreds and hundreds of experiences like that in the mission field.

THE MAORI RUGBY PLAYER

Elder McLaren brought a priest to see me at a fireside in new Zealand. The boy was a very large Maori who looked like he had the strength of many, and he had a question to ask. He had become one of the best rugby players in New Zealand, and had been invited to play with the All Blacks (a team that had just won the world championships). His question was what would happen to him if he played for the All Blacks and did not go on a mission.

I explained to him how I had had a scholarship to play basketball for Brigham Young University but had left on my mission after my freshman year, then returned to play basketball. I told him how I believed the Lord had blessed me so that I became a better ball player for having gone on a mission. It had to be his decision, and only God knew what would happen to him if he didn't go on a mission. He should fast and pray. He would get an answer, though he should be patient—the answer might not come on his first attempts to pray.

About two months later, he came to a missionary zone conference to ask another question. He had prayed about going on a mission and had received a vision in which he saw the Second Coming of the Savior. But he saw himself being burned to death. His question was "Why would the Lord burn me just because I didn't go on a mission?"

I told him to think about what he had seen. It appeared that if he failed to go on a mission, the lifestyle and temptations associated with a life of sports would lead him into sin, and he would not be worthy to receive all the ordinances necessary for salvation. Those sins would cause a burning.

By ten o'clock, the Lord had told him in a striking way what choice he should make.

ONE DEATH, TWO MIRACULOUSLY SPARED

Every once in a while, missionaries are killed in the mission field. My wife and I arrived on a Wednesday and were in the mission office by Thursday. We learned that two missionaries were going to be sent home by the former mission president, who told me, "You're now the mission president. Do what you want."

The next morning, I interviewed both missionaries, and they turned out to be good missionaries.

At two o'clock that afternoon, the telephone rang. An elder had been killed in a car accident in Te Kuiti, while riding in the car with three or four other elders and a young female member of the Church. The missionaries had left Hamilton to go to Te Kuiti to see the glowworm caves before they left. (The caves are one of the wonders of the world, I'm told.)

The missionaries had borrowed the girl's father's car, but she rolled the car, and the elder was killed. The other three in the car spent months in the hospital. We had to send one of them to finish his mission in Texas, because he needed some additional surgery.

The elders had been disobedient. They had left their area, and with a young girl, but does that justify the accident?

About four months later, an elder from Orem, Utah, arrived in the mission. His father had been my yardmaster when I was the blast furnace general foreman at Geneva Steel. We assigned the elder to a Samoan elder to work with the Samoans. The Samoan elder was very helpful to the Utah elder, who was a very shy young man.

One night about three months later, they were coming traveling on their bicycles down a hill in a rainstorm on their way home (they hadn't taken their umbrellas with them). As they came to an intersection, another car, which had the right-of-way, entered the intersection at the same time. We should have had two dead missionaries, but the car didn't even hit them. Their bikes rose in the air, the car passed under them, and they came back down on their bikes, completely unhurt. They were now so astonished that they fell off their bikes.

They called me from their apartment: "President Pedersen, you'll never guess what happened."

"Sure, I'll believe anything."

They described the "accident," then asked if I had ever heard of anything like that.

"Oh, I've heard of greater things than that. Here's what you do: You sit down and write your parents a letter, and then you write me."

The Samoan elder was terrified—he thought the end of the world had come. The other elder just thought it was a miracle.

So one of my missionaries died, but two were saved.

Afterword

I have never considered myself of any importance and thought I was of little significance. The experiences that I was blessed with came about by simple means and no great effort on my part other than simply believing in the scriptures and promises contained therein. I am grateful and humbled that the Lord has blessed me to participate in them and hear about them. All honor and glory belongs to Him. These experiences in this book have often blessed my life as much or more than they did those they affected more directly. Through these experiences and many others, I have come to know of the Lord's desire to bless all of his children with such encouraging and faith-promoting experiences.

Perhaps many of you have listened to my audio tapes or heard me speak. You may remember stories I told that are not contained in this book. Perhaps someday in the future I will have an opportunity to share more of these spiritual stories. They are a gift to me that I am happy to share. In the meantime, if any of you feel inspired or encouraged by what you have read, don't thank me, thank the Lord who is the source of all goodness.